LONDON UNDERGROUND GUIDE 2016

Written by Jason Cross
Edited by Nick Meskell
Design by Jason Prescott

Published by Train Crazy Publishing
© 2016 Train Crazy Publishing

All rights reserved. No part of this book may be reproduced or transmitted in any form or by any means, electronic or mechanical, including photocopying, scanning, recording or by any information storage and retrieval system, without written permission from the publisher.
Published by:
Train Crazy Publishing, Videoscene, PO Box 243, Lytham St Annes. FY8 9DE
email: sales@videoscene.co.uk

London Underground Guide 2016

Contents

Introduction 3
Changes Since the 2015 Guide Book 4

Useful Information, Facts & Tips 6

The Lines
- Bakerloo Line 12
- Central Line 16
- Jubilee Line 19
- Northern Line 23
- Piccadilly Line 27
- Victoria Line 30
- Waterloo & City Line 32
- Metropolitan Line 34
- Hammersmith & City Line 38
- Circle Line 41
- District Line 45

The Trains
D Stock 50
S Stock 53
1972 Stock 58
1973 Stock 60
1992 Stock 62
1995 Stock 65
1996 Stock 67
2009 Stock 69
Engineering Trains 70
Heritage Operations 78

A to Z of Underground Stations 80

Useful References 152

Underground Map *(fold out)* .... Inside Back cover

Introduction

Welcome to the 2016 London Underground Guide. Following on from our 2014 and 2015 London Underground Guide Books, this is the fully revised and re-written third edition updated to the beginning of 2016 and presented in a revised, larger format.

The London Underground is a complex system with a history that goes back over 150 years. This book is a guide to the Underground, and it aims to tell some of the history behind this fascinating system, while also describing the system as it is today with handy tips, a fleet list, an A-Z of stations, a look at engineering trains and a description of each line, all contained in a handy sized book that you can carry with you on the Underground.

The book has been written by an enthusiast and is aimed at fellow enthusiasts and anybody else who may have an interest in the London Underground. With a book of this size, it is impossible to describe every aspect of the Underground's operation in great detail. Information such as timetables, opening hours, the full range of ticketing options and which stations have step free access are not included. This information can be found via the official Transport for London website at www.tfl.gov.uk. Web links to pages that contain specific relevant information are included throughout this book.

The information contained in this book has come from official sources and from our own knowledge, research and observations. All of the pictures in this book were taken by the author, and included are several images taken from inside the driver's cab, which were taken with full official permission. The author would like to thank the many members of staff who have been most helpful with assistance and information that has contributed to this book, and also to Brian Hardy for his expert advice and proof reading skills. Please enjoy the book, and enjoy the Underground.

Jason Cross – Leicester

Content - The information provided in this book has been obtained from official sources as well as our observations, updated to 21 February 2016 (stock list is up to date to 31 January 2016).

Maps - Excluding the official underground map on the inside back cover (fold out), the individual line maps used in this publication are our own versions. These are to be used only as a rough guide. Connections to railway stations and other lines are not shown. Not all of the stations are open all of the day or at weekends and some do not have step-free access. Please use the official TfL map provided or check with TfL before travelling.

Front cover: A train of 1992 Tube Stock led by 91103 arrives at Bank with a Central Line service for Epping on 1 November 2015.

Rear cover: An S7 set pulled up at the Hammersmith terminus of the Circle and Hammersmith & City lines.

London Underground Guide 2016

Changes Since the 2015 Guide Book

Readers of the 2014 and 2015 guides will notice the change in format from a pocket sized book to A5 format. We listen to those who offer constructive criticism, and several of you told us that the size of the photographs and text was too small. So we have increased the size of the book and increased the number of pages to allow us to increase the font size and make the pictures larger. Although it is no longer pocket sized, it is still small enough to fit into a large pocket or a small bag. We hope you approve of the format change.

The introduction of new S Stock trains continues, and at the end of January 2016, there were still more than 30 S Stock trains to be delivered to the Underground (including an extra train that is to be built for the Croxley extension). With only the D Stock trains on the District Line still to be replaced, at the end of January 2016, just over half of the original fleet was still in service, although this will continue to reduce throughout 2016 as further trains of S Stock are delivered. It can be expected that some D Stock trains will see out most of 2016, and it might possibly be the beginning of 2017 before the class is totally eradicated from District Line services. Two D Stock units have been sent to Acton Works for conversion into a Rail Adhesion Train to replace the A Stock on the Metropolitan Line, and this train is expected to enter service for the 2016 autumn season. Some of the withdrawn D Stock vehicles have been sold on to Viva Rail who are planning to convert them to diesel power and refurbish them for potential future use on Network Rail.

The next stage in the upgrading of the Sub-Surface Railway (SSR) will be the re-signalling and introduction of automatic operation. The contract for this work is now with Thales, and a system largely similar to that already in place on the Jubilee and Northern lines is to be installed. The first S Stock train to operate in automatic mode ran on the Old Dalby test track on 16 November 2016. The new signalling will not go live in 2016, but work to install it will be taking place throughout the year. The S Stock fleet is also expected to have to return to Derby to have the signalling equipment installed and receive several other engineering modifications.

The planned introduction of the weekend 24 hour 'Night Tube' service on selected lines from 12 September 2015 did not happen. As this book went to press, no revised start date had been announced.

Throughout 2015, ticket offices at stations were closed, with passengers having to use ticket machines, Oyster Cards and contactless payments instead, or for other assistance seek the help of available staff or use a Help Point. TfL Visitor Centres were also opened at King's Cross, Victoria, Liverpool Street, Piccadilly Circus, Euston, Paddington, Gatwick Airport and Heathrow Airport.

Information

Information

USEFUL INFORMATION, FACTS AND TIPS

Train sizes, signalling, ticketing, and some interesting facts that will help readers as they go through the book.

Train Sizes – Tube or Surface

The London Underground has two different sizes of train. These are known as Surface Stock and Tube Stock. Although the London Underground seems to be now affectionately known as 'The Tube', this name is technically incorrect as not all lines are built to tube size. This is not helped by the fact that even Transport for London insist on calling the whole system by this name too.

There are four sub-surface lines, and seven tube lines. The earliest underground railways in London were built by the 'cut and cover' method. This is where a large trench was dug in the ground (usually down the centre of a road), side walls were built and railway tracks laid in the bottom of the trench, and then a roof was built over the top, and the road on the surface restored. This was a very disruptive method of construction which severely affected life on the surface while construction was taking place. These railways were built to generous dimensions however, and the trains that could operate on them could be the same height as trains that operate today on Network Rail. These lines are known as sub-surface lines, and the Metropolitan, Hammersmith & City, Circle and District lines are all built to this size.

Later lines were built at a much deeper level using 'Greathead Shields' (the 19th century equivalent of today's tunnel boring machines), and these are what we know today as the tube lines. The tube railways could be built without disturbing life on the surface, but the size of the trains was dictated by the overall diameter of the tube tunnel, which was much smaller than the size of the tunnels built by the 'cut and cover' method. The tube lines are made up of the Bakerloo, Central, Jubilee, Northern, Piccadilly, Victoria and Waterloo & City lines.

Surface Stock and Tube Stock standing side by side on Northfields Depot. The difference in height is clear to see. The train on the left is a train of S Stock, and the train on the right is 1973 Tube Stock.

Information

Preventing Surface Stock from Entering Tube Tunnels

There are a number of locations where full sized Surface Stock operates alongside the smaller Tube Stock. Where this occurs, there has to be a safeguard to prevent a train of Surface Stock from being wrongly routed into a tube tunnel. Between Hammersmith and Barons Court (eastbound Piccadilly), and between Hounslow Central and Hounslow West (westbound Piccadilly) are gantries from which three glass hoops are suspended above the track. They are of a length that allows a train of Tube Stock to pass beneath without making contact, but a taller train of Surface Stock would strike the tubes and smash them if one was to try and pass beneath. Inside the glass hoops is conductive paint which makes a circuit. Breaking the hoop would break the circuit and throw the signals to danger, which in turn would raise the associated train stop and the Surface Stock train would be stopped before it reached the tube tunnel. There used to be a similar gantry at Finchley Road on the Jubilee Line, but since the connection here between the Metropolitan Line and the Jubilee Line was removed, there is no longer any need for the glass hoops here and they have been removed, although the actual gantry is still in place. Any Surface Stock wrongly routed onto the Jubilee Line would now be tripped by fixed train stops at Neasden (the last physical connection between the two lines before tube tunnel can be reached).

It is also possible for a full height train from the Watford DC Line to be routed into the Bakerloo's tube tunnel at Queen's Park, but the train stop will only lower here if current is being drawn from the central (negative) conductor rail, and the London Overground class 378 units only collect power from the outer (positive) conductor rail.

The three glass hoops suspended from the gantry between Hammersmith and Barons Court can be seen in this photograph in the centre right portion of the picture.

Signals and Train Stops

Trains on the Metropolitan, Hammersmith & City, Circle, District, Bakerloo, Piccadilly and Waterloo & City lines are manually driven and controlled by colour light signals, which are fitted with a device called a train stop. A train stop is a 't' shaped piece of metal on the end of an arm which is raised when the signal displays a red aspect. Should a train pass that signal at danger, the plate will come into contact with a device on the train called a 'tripcock', which will release the air in the braking system and instigate a full emergency brake application (in the case of the newer S Stock trains, this is achieved by releasing the air in a valve which triggers the emergency brake application electronically). There are also several train stops around the system that are not attached to an adjacent signal, and which only lower if a train approaches it below a certain speed, such as on the approach to a terminus platform for example. Should a train approach one of these train stops too fast, it will not lower and the train will be 'tripped'.

Information

This view shows a signal displaying a red aspect. To the right of the right hand running rail can be seen a white plate raised above the height of the rail. This is the train stop, and should a train pass this signal while it is at danger, the tripcock on the train will strike the trainstop. When the signal clears, the train stop will lower to below the running rail, allowing the train's tripcock to pass over it. The train stop is always on the right hand side in the direction of travel.

Automatic Train Operation

There are several lines where passenger trains are operated automatically with Train Operators (The LU term for a train driver) operating the doors and pressing start buttons to start the train automatically. Across all lines, Train Operators still have to have the skills needed to drive a train manually and also have the skills and knowledge to be able to deal with a whole range of other potential incidents that could arise, regardless of whether they are working on an automatic line or a manually operated line. On automatic lines, the train will receive commands which will allow or forbid the train to proceed and set target speeds depending on the status of the track ahead. The signalling systems are either 'fixed block' or 'moving block', and the best way to describe the difference between the two is to think of a train departing from a station. With a 'fixed block' system, the line is divided up into sections (or 'blocks'). When a train is given a start command from a station, it looks at the block ahead, and if it is clear, the train can proceed. With a 'moving block' system, the line is not divided up into sections. Instead, each train has a safe zone around it, so when the train is given a start command, it can proceed provided it is not infringing on another train's safe zone. The safe zone around each train varies in size according to that train's speed. This means that as a train's speed decreases, the size of that train's safe zone also decreases in size, allowing trains to get as close to each other as is safely possible, thus making it possible to increase the number of trains on the line, and therefore increase the frequency of service. With 'moving block', it is possible, at busy times, sometimes to see a train enter a platform as soon as the previous train has departed it.

Both the Northern Line and the Jubilee Line operate using a 'moving block' system, this being the Thales 'Seltrac' Transmission Based Train Control (TBTC). This system sends commands to the train via a wire loop between the running rails. Unlike the systems employed by the Central and Victoria lines, the Northern and Jubilee lines do not require trackside signals.

The Central Line is fitted with a fixed block ATO/ATP system, with the Automatic Train Operation (ATO) driving the train and the Automatic Train Protection (ATP) picking up target speeds through codes transmitted through the track. There are colour light signals at the start of each block section, and these display either a green, white or red aspect. Green is go and is applicable to all trains, red is stop and is applicable to all trains, but white is go for a train in automatic mode, but stop for a train being driven manually.

8

Information

The Victoria Line is fitted with the fixed block Invensys (formerly Westinghouse) Distance to Go – Radio (DTG-R) system. ATO and ATP commands are transmitted via a radio link to the trains. Being radio based, it was possible to 'overlay' the DTG-R system on top of the original Westinghouse Automatic Train Control (ATC) system that was installed when the Victoria Line was opened. This allowed the new trains of 2009 Stock to operate alongside the old 1967 Stock during the period of transition. Once the 1967 Stock had been withdrawn, the old system was completely replaced by the DTG-R system, which allowed train frequencies to be increased. Should the ATP system fail, trains can still be moved manually in conjunction with trackside signals at a top speed of 15km/h. Should the ATO system fail, the train can still be driven manually at full line speed in accordance with the target speeds set by the ATP.

None of the automatically operated lines require the use of train stops, and so trains operating over them do not require tripcocks. There are occasions when engineering trains have to operate over these automatic lines, and to do so, they either have to be fitted with the relevant equipment to interface with the signalling, or operate under an 'incompatible train movement plan', which allows a train to move under its own power under strictly controlled conditions on a line for which it does not have the required signalling equipment on board.

Traction Current

The entire London Underground system is electrified using a standard four rail DC system (two running rails, and two electrified rails). One conductor rail is located centrally between the two running rails, and this is energised at -210V. There is then one conductor rail outside of the running rails which is energised at +420V, which gives a potential difference of 630V. The outer conductor rail can swap sides, but in stations, it is always on the opposite side to the platform edge except when a track has a platform on both sides. Where running is shared between the Underground and Network Rail, such as East Putney to Wimbledon, Gunnersbury to Richmond and Queen's Park (and Kilburn High Road) to Harrow & Wealdstone, the centre rail is bonded to the running rails. Work is underway to upgrade parts of the system to 750V supply.

Ticketing

The London Underground and other transport modes within London are split up into zones. Zone 1 is Central London, with zone 6 being the outer zone. There are also zones 7 to 9 which cover the Metropolitan Line north of Moor Park. The zones used and the number of zones passed through determine the price, with zone 1 being the most expensive.

The bulk of journeys on London Underground are made using an Oyster Card. This is a credit card sized plastic card, onto which users can pre-load season tickets and add credit with which travel can be paid for on a 'pay as you go' basis. An Oyster Card can be 'topped up' with credit at ticket machines in Underground stations, online via the Oyster website, in local shops, or it can be set to 'auto top up' direct from your bank account as soon as the amount of credit drops below £10. A 'Contactless' debit card can also be used in the same way as a 'pay as you go' card, with the advantage that you do not have to 'top up' as the system deducts the amount payable straight from the card owner's bank account. Both Oyster and 'Contactless' work by the user 'touching in' on the yellow Oyster pads on the gate line at the start of their journey, and then 'touching out' at the end of their journey. It may also be necessary to touch at an interchange point, and where this is the case, the readers are identifiable as they are pink in colour. The system will then charge the card with the cheapest possible fare. If multiple journeys are made during a day, the system will cap at a value that is determined by the number of zones used. The Oyster (and 'Contactless') system is time based, and it expects journeys to be made within a certain timescale. If the user goes over these time periods, the system will apply a maximum fare, and this additional charge also gets added onto the daily price cap. If used to make normal journeys, the system works well, but if you wish to pause to watch trains, you need to be aware of the time limits and make sure you touch out before going over one

9

Information

of the time limits. These time limits vary depending on the time of day and the number of zones you have passed through. Details of time limits can be found at: https://tfl.gov.uk/fares-and-payments/oyster/using-oyster/maximum-journey-times

If you wish to spend some time travelling on the Underground, and intend to linger to watch trains, and do not wish to keep having to worry about Oyster time limits, then it is recommended that a paper One Day Travelcard is purchased from a ticket machine at an Underground (or Network Rail) station. A zone 1 to 6 card will cover the entire Underground except for the Metropolitan north of Moor Park and costs just £12.10 off peak (Mon-Fri after 09:30, and all day Saturdays, Sundays and Bank Holidays) or £17.20 anytime (Mon-Fri for use before 09:30). If you intend to travel north of Moor Park, then a zone 1 to 9 card is available at £12.90 off peak or £21.70 anytime.

The use of paper single tickets purchased from ticket machines is not recommended, as a journey within zone 1 will cost £4.90 as a cash single, but just £2.40 with a card.

Oyster Cards, 'Contactless' and paper tickets are all valid on local Network Rail services, London Buses and Tramlink as well as the Underground.

Lamping Out

A procedure commonly known as 'lamping out' is used for the despatch of the last train of the day from each station. The Train Operator of the train concerned will not leave the platform until he receives a signal from a member of the platform staff. This signal usually takes the form of a green lamp which is clearly displayed so that the Train Operator can see it, and this is only displayed once any intending passengers have boarded. This operation is carried out to avoid passengers missing the last trains by seconds and is also part of the procedure for closing and securing the station at the end of traffic hours. At busy stations, the platform staff involved will often be in contact with the gateline staff to ensure that there are no further passengers on their way to the platform. This operation is seen in the picture being performed by Jack, a Customer Service Assistant (CSA) at King's Cross St Pancras as he 'lamps out' the last Chesham bound Metropolitan Line train of that day's traffic. This picture was taken with full permission.

The Lines

BAKERLOO LINE →

Bakerloo Line

Overview:

Route: Elephant & Castle to Harrow & Wealdstone

Route type: Tube

First section opened: Baker Street to Kennington Road (now Lambeth North) opened by the Baker Street & Waterloo Railway on 10 March 1906.

Method of train operation: Manually driven

Signalling: Colour light signals protected by train stops

Direction of route: Northbound / Southbound

Route length: 14.4 miles

Number of stations: 25

Trains: 1972 MkII Tube Stock with a few cars of 1972 MkI Tube Stock incorporated into the fleet.

Max number of trains required (peak times): 32

Depot: Stonebridge Park

Stabling points: Queen's Park / London Road / Elephant & Castle.

HISTORY

The Bakerloo Line began life as the Baker Street & Waterloo Railway and first opened between Baker Street and Kennington Road (now Lambeth North) on 10 March 1906, with the current southern terminus of the line at Elephant & Castle being reached on 5 August of the same year. The north end of the line was extended in stages, to Great Central (now Marylebone) on 27 March 1907, to Edgware Road on 15 June 1907, and then with backing from the Great Western Railway, to Paddington on 1 December 1913. The next section to Queen's Park opened in stages during the early part of 1915 with Queen's Park being reached on 11 February. Here the BS&WR met the London & North Western Railway's recently built London Euston to Watford Junction line (often referred to as the Watford DC Lines or the 'new' line), and BS&WR trains operated over LNWR tracks to Willesden Junction from 10 May 1915, and through to Watford Junction from 16 April 1917.

Further expansion of the Bakerloo was to come as part of the '1935-1940 New Works Programme' with a new section of tube tunnel from Baker Street to Finchley Road opening on 20 November 1939. The adjacent Metropolitan Railway route through Finchley Road to Baker Street, with trains from Aylesbury (and beyond), Chesham, Watford, Uxbridge and Stanmore all feeding into this two track section, had become rather congested, and the new tube tunnels were built to

Route diagram (stations):

- HARROW & WEALDSTONE
- KENTON
- SOUTH KENTON
- NORTH WEMBLEY
- WEMBLEY CENTRAL — *Stonebridge Park Depot*
- STONEBRIDGE PARK
- HARLESDEN
- WILLESDEN JUNCTION
- KENSAL GREEN
- QUEEN'S PARK — *Kilburn High Road (reversing moves without passengers)*
- KILBURN PARK
- MAIDA VALE
- WARWICK AVENUE
- PADDINGTON
- EDGWARE ROAD — *Connection with Jubilee Line (engineering trains only)*
- MARYLEBONE
- BAKER STREET
- REGENT'S PARK
- OXFORD CIRCUS
- PICCADILLY CIRCUS
- CHARING CROSS
- EMBANKMENT
- WATERLOO — *London Road Depot*
- LAMBETH NORTH
- ELEPHANT & CASTLE

Bakerloo

relieve that stretch of line by transferring the Stanmore branch trains to the Bakerloo and routing them through the new tunnels.

Baker Street had three platforms serving the Bakerloo after the tunnel section to Finchley Road opened, platform 7 was southbound serving trains from the Stanmore branch, platform 8 was southbound serving trains from the Watford / Queen's Park branch, and platform 9 was northbound serving both the Stanmore and Watford branches. It wasn't long before the single northbound platform became a bottleneck, and the solution came with the construction of a new platform serving the northbound Stanmore line. At the same time, a new tube tunnel route was built southwards from the Stanmore branch platforms to Charing Cross. This became the Jubilee Line, which opened on 1 May 1979 and saw the transfer of the Stanmore branch from the Bakerloo to the Jubilee. The junction between the Jubilee and the Bakerloo still exists at Baker Street, but today is only usually used by engineering trains which reach the Bakerloo from Ruislip Depot via the Jubilee Line.

This then left the Bakerloo with just the Elephant & Castle to Watford Junction route, but Bakerloo Line services were withdrawn north of Stonebridge Park in 1982, and then reinstated in 1984, but only as far as Harrow & Wealdstone, the current northern terminus of Bakerloo Line services.

An Elephant & Castle to Queen's Park service arrives at Warwick Avenue with unit 3563-4563-3463 leading on 1 March 2015.

THE ROUTE AND OPERATIONS

The southern terminus of the Bakerloo Line is at Elephant & Castle, which makes it unique on the Underground for having its terminus so close to central London. Under normal operating conditions during the day, all southbound trains run through to Elephant & Castle, while in the northbound direction, roughly half of all trains terminate at Queen's Park, with roughly 20% terminating at Stonebridge Park and approximately 30% running through to the northern terminus of the Bakerloo Line at Harrow & Wealdstone.

From Harrow & Wealdstone to Queen's Park, the Bakerloo shares its tracks with the Watford DC electric service, which is today operated by London Overground class 378 units that operate between London Euston and Watford Junction. The signalling on this section of the line is controlled

Bakerloo Line

3251-4251-4351-3351 leads a train out of 21 road at Queen's Park into the station to form the 2330 service to Waterloo, where it will terminate and continue empty into London Road Sidings. 29 January 2015. The upper case destination blinds have since been replaced by lower case blinds.

by Network Rail, but it still has London Underground train stops at each signal and both the 1972 Tube Stock and the class 378's are fitted with tripcocks. The Watford DC Line is also fitted throughout with Network Rail's AWS and TPWS systems, including the section used by Bakerloo Line trains, which allows other main line trains to use the route (Network Rail test trains and the autumn railhead treatment train, for example). Bakerloo Line trains are not compatible with AWS or TPWS. Train stops are fitted to all signals on the Watford DC line between Harrow & Wealdstone and Kilburn High Road, which is the first station south of Queen's Park towards London Euston. London Underground trains can run out-of-service to Kilburn High Road to reverse at times of disruption, and the central conductor rail is in place to just beyond the south end of the station platforms for this purpose. It is rare to see a Bakerloo Line train run to Kilburn High Road in daylight, but there are a number of night time paths that occasionally run, especially during icy weather, when they shuttle between Kilburn High Road and Harrow & Wealdstone in order to keep the conductor rails free of ice. These trains also occasionally operate to prevent the build up of rust on the centre conductor rail between Queen's Park and Kilburn High Road.

Queen's Park can be considered to be the hub of the Bakerloo Line. It is where a high proportion of trains from Central London reverse, and it is also where the Bakerloo Line and the Watford DC Lines come together at Queen's Park Junction, which is situated at the north end of the Queen's Park North Shed. This junction also forms the boundary between London Underground and Network Rail. Trains that reverse at Queen's Park do so by running into either 22 or 23 road in the North Shed. Northbound Bakerloo trains that continue beyond Queen's Park pass through the North Shed on road 21, and southbound Bakerloo trains from north of Queen's Park pass through road 24. Outside of traffic hours, all four roads (21-24) can be used to stable trains. There is also a South Shed at Queen's Park which holds up to four trains. Other locations where trains stable are in the two sidings beyond the platforms at Elephant & Castle, and in London Road Sidings. This latter location is situated in Lambeth and is reached by a single track spur and scissors crossover to the north of Lambeth North station. Eleven trains usually stable here at night, and some of these trains finish

Bakerloo Line

their duties with Waterloo as their destination. Here the train will terminate and proceed empty to London Road. Under normal circumstances, this is the only time a destination other than Elephant & Castle can be seen on the front of a southbound train south of Queen's Park.

The rest of the Bakerloo Line's fleet stable at the main depot at Stonebridge Park, which is situated to the north of Stonebridge Park station and is reached by a spur off of the DC Lines at the north end of the platforms. A number of trains also reverse here during traffic hours and they usually do so by running into either road 21 or 22 in the entrance to the depot.

South of Queen's Park, the Bakerloo dives down into tube tunnel alongside the South Shed, and then remains below ground all the way to the southern terminus at Elephant & Castle. En route, it serves the West End and the mainline termini of Paddington, Marylebone, Charing Cross and Waterloo.

The Bakerloo is currently operated by a fleet of 1972 MkII Tube Stock (see page 58). There are a number of 1972 MkI Tube Stock cars incorporated into the fleet which are highlighted in the stock list on page 59. Since the withdrawal of the C Stock in 2014, the 1972 Tube Stock is now the oldest passenger stock in regular service on the London Underground. Bakerloo Line trains are allocated numbers in the series 201 to 253. This number is displayed on the front of trains on a digital display in the cab window. The maximum number of trains in service at any one time occurs late in the morning peak on weekdays when 32 trains are scheduled to be in service.

First trains:

0537 Elephant & Castle to Harrow & Wealdstone 0627 (Mon-Sat)
0716 Elephant & Castle to Harrow & Wealdstone 0806 (Sun)
0538 Harrow & Wealdstone to Elephant & Castle 0628 (Mon-Sat)
0723 Harrow & Wealdstone to Elephant & Castle 0812 (Sun)

Last trains:

2346 Elephant & Castle to Harrow & Wealdstone 0036 (Mon-Sat)
2337 Elephant & Castle to Harrow & Wealdstone 0026 (Sun)
2354 Harrow & Wealdstone to Elephant & Castle 0043 (Mon-Sat)
2313 Harrow & Wealdstone to Elephant & Castle 0001 (Sun)

Note: *The above trains are the first and last trains to travel the full length of the line. There are other shorter workings before and after those listed above.*

3259-4259-4359-3359 leads the 0018 Harrow & Wealdstone to Queen's Park service into Harlesden on 30 January 2015. This is a short working that gets this train to Queen's Park where it will stable for the night (in the South Shed).

CENTRAL LINE →

Central Line

Overview:

Route: West Ruislip and Ealing Broadway to Hainault, Woodford and Epping

Route Type: Tube

First section opened: Shepherd's Bush to Bank, opened (to the public) by the Central London Railway on 30 July 1900.

Method of train operation: Automatic

Signalling: ATO/ATP

Direction of route: Eastbound / Westbound (plus inner rail and outer rail Leytonstone to Woodford via Newbury Park)

Route length: 46 miles

Number of stations: 49

Trains: 1992 Stock.

Max number of trains required (peak times): 79

Depots: Hainault and Ruislip

Stabling points: White City / Loughton / Woodford.

HISTORY

The first part of the Central London Railway was opened by the Prince of Wales on 27 June 1900 between Shepherd's Bush and Bank, with opening to the public following on 30 July of the same year. To begin with, the line was operated by electric locomotives, but these machines caused too many vibrations, plus there was the added complication of reversing at each terminus, and by 1903, they had been replaced by motor carriages. The first extension was to Wood Lane which was situated on a balloon shaped loop to the west of the original terminus at Shepherd's Bush. This new station was opened to serve the Franco British Exhibition that was taking place at Wood Lane. Trains were turned on this loop ready for their journey back towards Bank without the need for the driver to change ends. When Wood Lane bound trains departed from Shepherd's Bush, the westbound track passed over the top of the eastbound track with trains then travelling around the loop in a counter-clockwise direction. When the line was extended further west in 1920 over the tracks of the Great Western Railway's Ealing & Shepherd's Bush Railway to Ealing Broadway, trains came off the Wood Lane loop on the right hand side, an arrangement that still exists today and can be witnessed at White City station where right hand running prevails. A flyover close to Wormwood

16

Central Line

A train of 1992 Stock with 91165 on the rear departs from number 21 siding at Woodford to form a Woodford to Ealing Broadway service on 7 March 2015. This train will run clockwise round the Hainault loop via Chigwell and Newbury Park.

A train of 1992 Tube Stock led by 91237 arrives at Lancaster Gate with a westbound Central Line service on 18 October 2015.

Scrubs prison switches the tracks back to left hand running. At the east end of the line, an extension from Bank to Liverpool Street opened on 28 July 1912.

The '1935-1940 New Works Programme' included plans to extend the Central Line at both ends. Both of these extensions were delayed by the war. At the west end, a new line ran to West Ruislip which diverged from the Ealing Broadway line at North Acton Junction. This opened to Greenford in 1947, and to West Ruislip on 21 November 1948. At the east end, the Central Line was extended partly in new tube tunnel, but mostly over former LNER tracks to Hainault, Woodford, Epping and Ongar. Work on the tunnel sections between Liverpool Street and Stratford, Stratford and Leyton and Leytonstone and Newbury Park were largely complete when war broke out, and the latter section was converted into an underground secret aircraft components factory. The partially complete Bethnal Green station was used as an air raid shelter and was the scene of a terrible disaster that resulted in the loss of 173 lives (see page 87). After the war, work resumed on the extension, and the first section to open was between Liverpool Street and Stratford on 4 December 1946. This was followed by the next section to Leytonstone on 5 May 1947. Part of this section was originally opened by the Eastern Counties Railway on 22 August 1856, so actually pre-dates the rest of the Underground. For a while, Central Line trains could be seen alongside LNER steam trains at Leytonstone until the next section to Woodford was transferred over from the LNER to the Central Line on 14 December 1947. On the same day, the new tunnel section from Leytonstone to Newbury Park also opened. The Newbury Park to Hainault section saw the last LNER steam train services in November 1947, and from December 1947, Central Line trains used the line to run empty between Newbury Park and the new Central Line depot at Hainault. Central Line passenger services began

17

Central Line

over this section on 31 May 1948. Beyond Hainault, the line forms a loop, joining up with the Epping line to the east of Woodford, and this saw the introduction of Central Line trains from 21 November 1948. On the same date, the next section east of Woodford as far as Loughton became part of the Central Line. The final section from Loughton to Epping and Ongar became part of the Central Line from 25 September 1949. Initially, the Epping to Ongar section was not electrified, and although part of London Underground from the same date, services were operated by a hired in British Railways steam train and carriages until 1957 when the line was electrified. Low patronage of the Epping to Ongar section eventually led to the closure of the line on 30 September 1994. Thankfully, the line has survived and is now a preserved railway (see eorailway.co.uk). The line is still connected to the Central Line at Epping, with E&OR trains able to run to within a few hundred yards of the Central Line.

THE ROUTE AND OPERATIONS

The Central Line runs across the middle of London serving the West End, the shopping district around Oxford Street and the City of London. At either end, it runs out into the suburbs and reaches out as far as Epping in the east and West Ruislip in the west. The journey from Epping to West Ruislip is the longest journey possible on the Underground without changing trains, and takes 85 minutes. The trains used on the Central Line are 8-car trains of 1992 Tube Stock built by ABB in Derby (see page 62). The whole of the Central Line is operated automatically using a system of ATO and ATP (see page 8).

Service patterns are a mix of trains that operate over the full length of the line together with trains that work shorter journeys in order to concentrate a larger number of trains through Central London. The majority of trains operate between Epping and West Ruislip, between Ealing Broadway and Hainault (via Newbury Park) and between Ealing Broadway and Woodford (via Hainault). The bulk of shorter workings run between White City and Newbury Park and between Loughton and Northolt. There are also a number of trains that reverse at Debden and North Acton during peak hours. In addition, should the service be disrupted for any reason, there are a number of locations where trains can be reversed which currently do not have trains timetabled to reverse there. These include reversing sidings at Liverpool Street, Marble Arch and the closed British Museum station (situated to the west of Holborn), and crossovers at Queensway and Bethnal Green.

Outside of traffic hours, trains stable in sidings at Woodford and Loughton at the east end, and at White City at the west end, as well as at the two main depots at Hainault and Ruislip. Some trains entering or leaving Ruislip and Hainault depots start or finish their journeys at Ruislip Gardens and Grange Hill respectively. There are also several trains that stable in Loughton sidings which start and finish their day by running in service between Loughton and Epping and vice versa. The maximum number of trains required in service is 79, which occurs during the morning peak.

First trains:

0510 Epping to West Ruislip 0634 (Mon-Sat)
0642 Epping to West Ruislip 0807 (Sun)
0523 West Ruislip to Epping 0646 (Mon-Sat)
0641 West Ruislip to Epping 0805 (Sun)

Last trains:

2345 Epping to West Ruislip 0110 (Mon-Sat)
2257 Epping to West Ruislip 0028 (Sun)
2353 West Ruislip to Epping 0116 (Mon-Sat)
2258 West Ruislip to Epping 0022 (Sun)

Note: The above trains are the first and last trains to travel the full length of the line. There are other shorter workings before and after those listed above.

JUBILEE LINE →

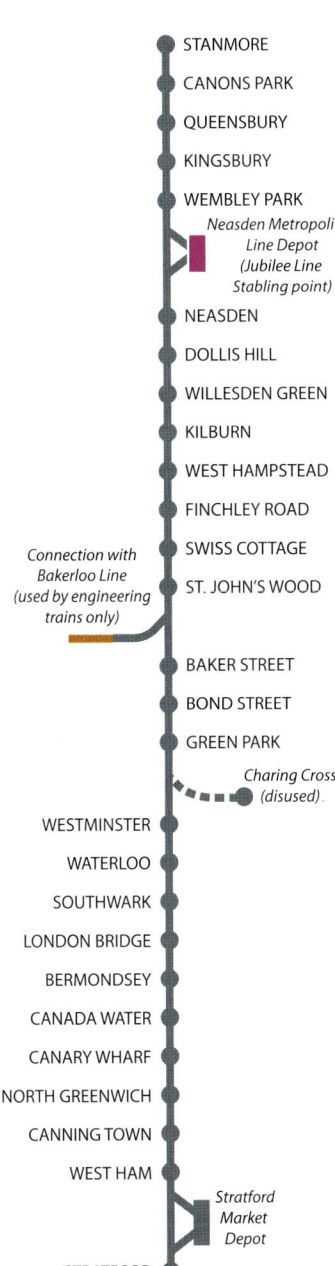

Jubilee Line

Overview:

Route: Stanmore to Stratford

Route type: Tube

First Section Opened: Stanmore to Wembley Park, opened by the Metropolitan Railway on 10 December 1932.

Method of train operation: Automatic

Signalling: Transmission Based Train Control 'moving block' system (TBTC)

Direction of route: Northbound / Southbound between Stanmore and Green Park, and Eastbound / Westbound between Green Park and Stratford.

Route length: 22.5 miles

Number of stations: 27

Trains: 1996 Tube Stock

Max number of trains required (peak times): 58

Depot: Stratford Market

Stabling points: Stanmore / Neasden

HISTORY

Although the Jubilee Line was opened in 1979, parts of the line pre-date this, so the history of the line goes back much further - 100 years in fact - to 1879, as the section of the Metropolitan Railway between Finchley Road and Wembley Park, over which the Jubilee Line runs today alongside the Metropolitan, was opened in 1879 and 1880. This piece of history really belongs to the Metropolitan though, as this line was built as part of a main line from Central London reaching out to Chesham, and eventually Amersham, Aylesbury, Uxbridge and Watford. It was the opening of a branch to Stanmore in Middlesex by the Metropolitan Railway on 10 December 1932, and the additional traffic that was generated by it, that can be viewed as the start of a chain of events that eventually led to the creation of what we know today as the Jubilee Line.

The Stanmore branch joined the Metropolitan Railway's main line at Wembley Park, and trains from Stanmore shared tracks between there and the City with other Metropolitan Railway services which ran to and from Uxbridge, Watford, Chesham, Amersham, Aylesbury and beyond. With so many trains running to and from the City, all of which had to pass through the two-track tunnel section between Finchley Road and Baker Street, the line became very congested. In order to relieve this, as part of the '1935-1940 New Works Programme', a new two track railway was built in tube tunnel from the Bakerloo Line at Baker Street to Finchley Road. This opened on 20 November

19

Jubilee Line

The disused former terminus of the Jubilee Line at Charing Cross with an engineering train hauled by battery locomotive L48 stabled in platform 4. (Photograph was taken with permission)

Jubilee Line

1939, and also saw the transfer of the Stanmore branch from the Metropolitan to the Bakerloo. The two intermediate stations on this new line at Swiss Cottage and St John's Wood also resulted in the closure of the three Metropolitan Line stations at Swiss Cottage, Marlborough Road and Lords, giving Metropolitan Line trains a faster run into and out of the City.

The Bakerloo operated for many years with its two northern branches to Stanmore and Watford Junction with a junction at Baker Street until this too began to suffer from congestion. This was not helped by the fact that in the southbound direction, trains from the Stanmore and Watford Junction branches each had their own separate platforms at Baker Street, but northbound trains to both branches had to share one platform. Relief was to come in the shape of an additional northbound platform to be constructed as part of a new tube line into Central London. In 1971, construction began on the new 'Fleet Line', as the Jubilee was to be known originally, the name being changed in 1977 as recognition of HM Queen Elizabeth II's Silver Jubilee. The new line ran through Bond Street and Green Park to a new terminus at Charing Cross where interchange with British Rail and the Bakerloo and Northern lines was provided. Opening on 1 May 1979, the new Jubilee Line also took over the Stanmore branch from the Bakerloo on the same day, reducing the Bakerloo to operate between Watford Junction and Elephant & Castle only, while the Jubilee Line operated between Stanmore and Charing Cross. The former branch junction at Baker Street is still in place, and forms a link between the two lines which is used today by engineering trains travelling between Ruislip Depot and the Bakerloo Line.

With the development of the Docklands area in the east end of London came the need for improved transport links. The only Underground line to serve the heart of Docklands was the East London Line (now part of the London Overground network), but this did not run directly into the City. An extension to the Jubilee Line was built which passed through Westminster, Waterloo, North Greenwich, Canary Wharf, Canning Town and West Ham to Stratford. This new line opened in stages during 1999, with through running over the entire route from 20 November 1999. Known as the Jubilee Line Extension (JLE), this new line branched off the existing line to the south of Green Park, thus missing out the Charing Cross terminus which closed on 19 November 1999. Charing Cross can still be used to reverse trains (out of service), to stable engineering trains and is also used for filming purposes.

THE ROUTE AND OPERATIONS

The Jubilee Line is operated by a fleet of 1996 Tube Stock trains (see page 67) which are formed of 7 cars. These trains operate in automatic mode using the Thales Transmission Based Control System (see page 8). The TBTC system was introduced in two stages, stage one between Dollis Hill and Stratford (including Charing Cross) on 29 December 2010, with stage two between Dollis Hill and Stanmore going live on 26 June 2011.

The main depot is at Stratford Market. It was constructed as part of the JLE project. Prior to the building of the JLE, the Jubilee Line's main depot was Neasden which it shared with the Metropolitan Line. The Jubilee Line now only uses Neasden as a stabling location along with a fan of sidings alongside Stanmore station. Jubilee Line trains coming into service from Neasden depot can reach the main Jubilee tracks via an underpass at the north end of the depot (which can also be used by Metropolitan Line trains to join the northbound Metropolitan Line tracks), but at the south end, they cross over the southbound Metropolitan track on a flat junction. Engineering trains travelling to or from the Jubilee Line also use this junction. It is possible that a wrongly routed Metropolitan Line train could end up on Jubilee Line tracks, and as a precaution there are a number of fixed train stops around Neasden station that would 'trip' a Metropolitan Line train and bring it to a standstill should this happen. Somewhat confusingly, the Jubilee Line is a northbound / southbound railway between Stanmore and Green Park, but the JLE between Green Park and Stratford is an eastbound / westbound railway. This can be confusing to passengers, who may board a westbound train on the JLE, but alight from a northbound train further up the line (and vice versa).

Jubilee Line

An eastbound Jubilee Line train is seen during its station stop at Canada Water, where the platform edge doors (PEDs) can be clearly seen.

On the JLE, all of the below ground stations have platform edge doors (PEDs). The doors remain closed until a train is stationary in the platform, at which point the PEDs open simultaneously with the doors on the train.

The majority of trains operate over the full length of the line between Stanmore and Stratford. There are, however, several shorter workings designed to concentrate more trains on the central section of the route. The bulk of short workings reverse at either Wembley Park, Willesden Green or North Greenwich. It is also possible to reverse trains at Canary Wharf, West Hampstead, Green Park (via Charing Cross), Waterloo and London Bridge, but reversing at these locations only occurs during service disruption. Some trains coming out of or going into Stratford Market depot enter or leave passenger service at West Ham.

The maximum number of trains in service at one time is 58, and this occurs both in the morning and evening peaks on a Monday to Friday. This allows a peak service of 30 trains per hour in both directions to be operated.

First trains:
0515 Stratford to Stanmore 0611 (Mon-Sat)
0709 Stratford to Stanmore 0806 (Sun)
0523 Stanmore to Stratford 0622 (Mon-Sat)
0653 Stanmore to Stratford 0753 (Sun)

Last trains:
0011 Stratford to Stanmore 0109 (Mon-Sat)
2337 Stratford to Stanmore 0034 (Sun)
0013 Stanmore to Stratford 0111 (Mon-Sat)
2326 Stanmore to Stratford 0025 (Sun)

Note: The above trains are the first and last trains to travel the full length of the line. There are other shorter workings before and after those listed above. Earlier trains through Central London to Stratford on a Monday to Saturday are offered by the 0505 and 0522 ex Wembley Park, and the 0512 and 0532 ex Neasden (which enter service from the south end of Neasden Depot) which run ahead of the first train from Stanmore.

NORTHERN LINE ➔

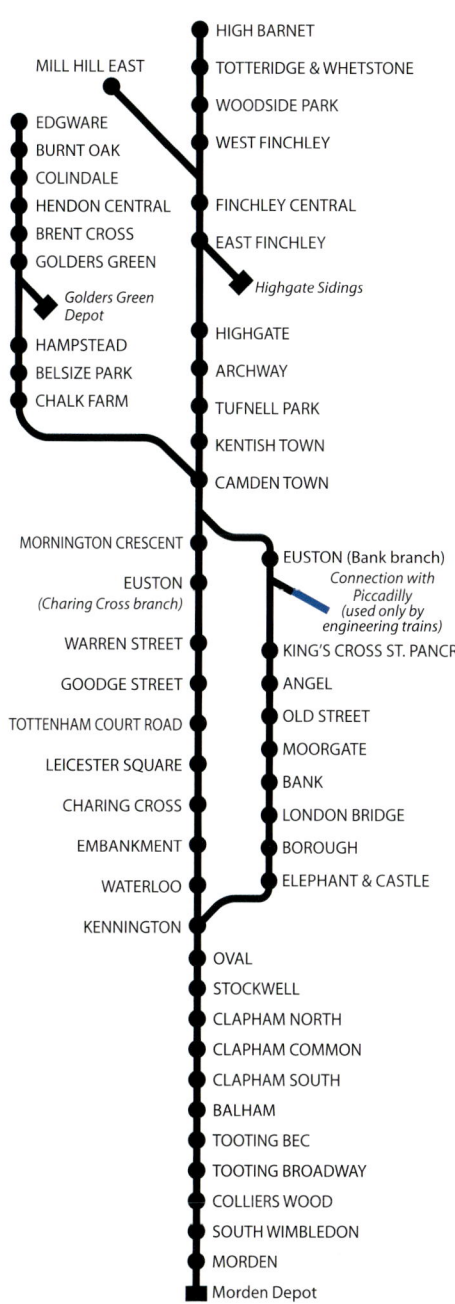

Northern Line

Overview:

Route: Edgware, High Barnet and Mill Hill East to Morden via Charing Cross or Bank

Route type: Tube

First section opened: King William Street to Stockwell, opened by the City & South London Railway on 18 December 1890.

Method of train operation: Automatic

Signalling: Transmission Based Train Control 'moving block' system (TBTC)

Direction of route: Northbound / Southbound.

Route length: 36 miles

Number of stations: 50

Trains: 1995 Tube Stock

Max number of trains required (peak times): 96

Depots: Golders Green and Morden

Stabling points: Edgware / High Barnet / Highgate

HISTORY

The City & South London Railway (C&SLR) opened the world's first deep level tube railway between King William Street and Stockwell in 1890. It was also London's first electric railway (as the earlier sub surface lines were still powered by steam at this time). The Prince of Wales (later to become King Edward VII) performed an official opening ceremony on 4 November 1890, but opening to the public did not follow until 18 December of the same year. Early trains were locomotive hauled with the passenger stock having high backed seating and small windows, earning them the nickname 'padded cells'. A locomotive and a passenger carriage can be found on display in the London Transport Museum. The first extension of the line was northwards to Moorgate Street which opened on 25 February 1900, and this line bypassed the King William Street terminus making it redundant. Further extensions followed, southwards to Clapham Common (opened 3 June 1900), northwards to Angel (opened 17 November 1901) and northwards again to Euston (opened on 12 May 1907).

On 22 June 1907, the Charing Cross, Euston &

Northern Line

A Kennington to High Barnet service arrives into Euston (Charing Cross branch) led by 51606 on 29 August 2015.

Hampstead Railway (CCE&HR) opened a line from Charing Cross to Camden Town, where the line split with one branch going to Highgate (this station is today called Archway) and one branch going to Golders Green. This line became known as the 'Hampstead Tube'. The line was extended at the south end one stop to Charing Cross (Embankment) on 6 April 1914. At the same time, Charing Cross was renamed Charing Cross (Strand). Charing Cross (Embankment) was a single platform built on a balloon shaped loop so that trains could return north without the need for the driver to change ends.

The C&SLR, being the first tube line, had built its tunnels to a diameter that it had deemed to be large enough at that time. Subsequently built tube lines had been built to a slightly larger diameter, and the C&SLR needed to enlarge its tunnels. Moorgate to Clapham Common was closed between 28 November 1923 and 1 December 1924, and Moorgate to Euston was closed between August 1922 and April 1924 to allow the tunnels to be enlarged. The reopening of the Moorgate to Euston section also coincided with the opening of an extension from Euston to Camden Town where the C&SLR joined up with the Hampstead & Highgate Line (previously known as the CCE&HR). This extension opened on 20 April 1924.

Golders Green ceased to be a terminus when the line was extended northwards towards Edgware, and the first section to Hendon opened on 19 November 1923. Edgware was reached on 18 August 1924. At the south end of the Hampstead & Highgate Line, the line was extended beyond the balloon shaped loop at Charing Cross (the station known today as Embankment), to join the C&SLR at Kennington. This opened on 13 September 1926, the same day as an extension from Clapham Common to Morden was opened by the C&SLR. On 1 July 1933, the C&SLR and the Hampstead & Highgate Line were combined to become the Edgware, Highgate & Morden Line of the London Passenger Transport Board. This was renamed to the Morden-Edgware Line in 1934, and then finally, on 28 August 1937, the name was changed again to the Northern Line.

The '1935-1940 New Works Programme' saw the opening on 3 July 1939 of an extension of the Highgate branch to East Finchley. From there, the Northern Line took over the LNER tracks through to High Barnet with tube trains working through from 14 April 1940. The Northern also took over

Northern Line

the first part of the LNER's Edgware branch between Finchley Central and Mill Hill East. The main purpose of this branch was to serve the barracks close to Mill Hill East station and it opened to tube trains on 18 May 1941. The line beyond Mill Hill East to Edgware was never electrified and was used for freight traffic until closure in 1964.

Also part of the Northern Line's history is the Great Northern & City Railway. This was opened between Finsbury Park and Moorgate on 14 February 1904. It was taken over by the Metropolitan Railway on 1 September 1913, and was then operated as part of the Northern Line from 1939. The line was closed between Finsbury Park and Drayton Park on 3 October 1964 to allow for the construction of the (then) new Victoria Line. This was followed by the section between Moorgate and Old Street, which closed on 6 September 1975, with the remaining section between Old Street and Drayton Park closing on 4 October 1975. The line later re-opened as part of British Rail operated by class 313 EMUs. The line is today still a part of Network Rail and is still served by class 313 EMUs which operate between Moorgate and Stevenage / Welwyn Garden City.

THE ROUTE AND OPERATIONS

The Northern Line is operated by a fleet of 1995 Tube Stock built by Alsthom (see page 65). All trains are formed of 6 cars and operate in automatic mode using the Thales Transmission Based Train Control System (TBTC). The TBTC system was introduced in stages with the whole line being converted by 1 June 2014. Any train using the Kennington loop becomes turned, so the 'A' end of trains can face either north or south.

There are two main depots, at Golders Green and Morden. Both of these depots are operated by Alsthom, who look after the Northern's fleet as part of a supply and maintenance contract. Morden Depot is situated to the south of Morden station and is the most southerly location reached by the Underground. There are also three stabling points at Edgware, High Barnet and Highgate. The latter is located on the former LNER line to Finsbury Park to the south of East Finchley station and is accessed via the two tracks that pass through the centre platforms at East Finchley.

The Northern Line is unique in having two branches through Central London which serve the City of London (Bank branch) and the West End (Charing Cross branch). The two branches separate at Camden Town in the north and at Kennington in the south. Camden Town is really the hub of the Northern and is where the High Barnet, Edgware, Bank and Charing Cross branches all come together, and it is possible for trains from either the High Barnet or Edgware branches to continue via either the Charing Cross or Bank branches and vice versa.

Most of the Northern is in tube tunnel. At the south end, Morden station is located in a cutting with trains entering tunnel just a short distance from the north end of the platform, with the first few hundred yards of this tunnel being 'cut and cover' before it becomes tube tunnel. Travelling north, the Northern emerges into daylight on the approach to Golders Green on the Edgware branch, and on the approach to East Finchley on the High Barnet branch. A train travelling between the High Barnet branch and Morden via Bank (and vice versa), will be in tunnel for just over 17 miles, the longest continuous tunnel on the Underground.

The bulk of services operate between Edgware and Morden (via Bank), Edgware and Kennington (via Charing Cross), High Barnet and Morden (via Bank) and High Barnet and Kennington (via Charing Cross). The Mill Hill East branch operates as a shuttle service to and from Finchley Central for most of the day, but does have a number of through trains to and from both Morden and Kennington during the morning and evening peaks. Mill Hill East is also served by through trains at the start and end of traffic. At the start of traffic, a number of trains leave Highgate Sidings and work in passenger service from East Finchley to Mill Hill East, and then form a southbound service from there. At the end of traffic, a number of trains operate through from Morden or Kennington to Mill Hill East, and then form a service to East Finchley from there and then run empty into Highgate Sidings. The bulk of trains on the Charing Cross branch reverse at Kennington via a balloon shaped loop which enables them to reverse without the need for the driver to change ends. Trains arrive from the north

Northern Line

in platform 2, de-train, then proceed around the loop and arrive into platform 1 to form a northbound service. There is also a reversing siding which can be reached by trains from either the Bank branch or the Charing Cross branch, and trains exiting the siding can also access both branches. During peak hours, and at the start and end of traffic, there are a number of Charing Cross branch trains which run to and from Morden. There are of course variations at the start and end of service which see trains starting and ending their journeys at Golders Green and East Finchley in order to exit / enter Golders Green Depot and Highgate Sidings respectively. A maximum of 96 trains are needed for service in both the morning and evening peaks.

First trains:

0515 Morden to High Barnet 0617 – via Charing Cross (Mon-Sat)
0518 Morden to Edgware 0622 – via Bank (Mon-Sat)
0656 Morden to High Barnet 0805 – via Bank (Sun)
0659 Morden to Edgware 0801 – via Charing Cross (Sun)
0522 Edgware to Morden 0625 – via Charing Cross (Mon-Sat)
0522 High Barnet to Morden 0629 – via Bank (Mon-Sat)
0655 Edgware to Morden 0801 – via Bank (Sun)
0654 High Barnet to Kennington 0734 – via Charing Cross (Sun)

Last trains:

0005 Morden to High Barnet 0115 – via Bank (Mon-Sat)
0005 Kennington to Edgware 0113 – via Charing Cross (Mon-Sat)
2310 Morden to High Barnet 0019 – via Bank (Sun)
2337 Kennington to Edgware 0017 – via Charing Cross (Sun)
0000 High Barnet to Morden 0108 – via Bank (Mon-Sat)
0001 Edgware to Morden 0103 – via Charing Cross (Mon-Sat)
2308 High Barnet to Morden 0019 – via Bank (Sun)
2310 Edgware to Morden 0015 – via Charing Cross (Sun)

Note: The above trains are the first and last trains to serve the entire length of the Edgware and High Barnet branches, as well as the Bank and Charing Cross branches. There are other shorter workings before and after those listed above.

51543 is seen on the rear of train 021, the 0702 East Finchley to Mill Hill East on Sunday 27 December 2015. The train is departing platform 2 at East Finchley, having arrived empty from Highgate Sidings. Throughout most of the day, northbound and southbound trains use the two outer platforms, 1 and 4, with the two inner platforms seen here not used.

26

Piccadilly Line

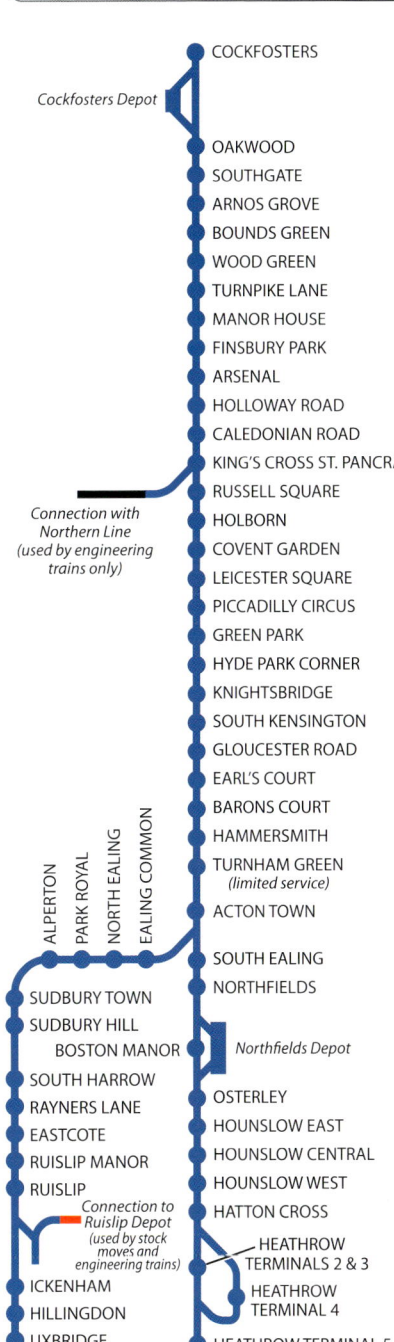

Overview:

Route: Cockfosters to Heathrow and Uxbridge.

Route type: Tube

First section opened: Finsbury Park to Hammersmith opened by the Great Northern, Piccadilly & Brompton Railway on 15 December 1906.

Method of train operation: Manually driven

Signalling: Colour light signals protected by train stops

Direction of route: Eastbound / Westbound.

Route length: 44.3 miles

Number of stations: 53

Trains: 1973 Tube Stock

Max number of trains required (peak times): 78

Depots: Cockfosters and Northfields

Stabling points: Arnos Grove / South Harrow / Uxbridge

HISTORY

The Great Northern, Piccadilly & Brompton Railway opened its railway between Finsbury Park and Hammersmith on 15 December 1906. This was followed on 30 November 1907 by the opening of the short branch between Holborn and Strand (later to be renamed Aldwych). Services were extended westwards from Hammersmith using the centre pair of tracks between there and Acton Town to give a non-stop service parallel to the District, an arrangement that still exists to this day. The Piccadilly took over District services to South Harrow from 4 July 1932, with the District still providing the service from there to Uxbridge until the Piccadilly also took over this section from 23 October 1933. The Piccadilly also took over the Hounslow branch from the District, with Piccadilly Line trains running to Northfields from 9 January 1933, and to Hounslow West from 13 March 1933. District Line trains continued to serve the Hounslow branch at rush hour alongside those of the Piccadilly Line until they were finally withdrawn in 1964.

At the east end, the Piccadilly was extended beyond Finsbury Park to Cockfosters. This line opened in stages during 1932 and 1933 with the first stage to Arnos Grove opening on 19 September 1932, to Enfield West (later renamed Oakwood) on 13 March 1933 and finally to Cockfosters on 31 July 1933.

27

Piccadilly Line

An extension from Hounslow West to Hatton Cross was opened on 19 July 1975. This was the first section of an extension to serve Heathrow Airport, and the next section to Heathrow Central was opened on 16 December 1977. Expansion of the airport saw further extension of the Piccadilly and a new station on a single track loop called Heathrow Terminal 4 was opened on 12 April 1986. At the same time, Heathrow Central was renamed Heathrow Terminals 1,2,3 and it was transformed from a terminus station into a through station. A new terminus serving Heathrow Terminal 5 was opened on a short branch to the west of Heathrow Terminals 1,2,3 (since renamed to Heathrow Terminals 2 & 3), on 27 March 2008.

The Holborn to Aldwych branch was closed on 30 September 1994 (the same day as the Central Line's Epping to Ongar line). The branch is still in situ and is used for training and filming purposes.

Two trains of 1973 Tube Stock pass at Hatton Cross on the Heathrow extension on 29 August 2015. The train on the left is a double ended unit (distinguished by the inter car barrier fixings on the corners of the cab).

THE ROUTE AND OPERATIONS

The Piccadilly Line is operated by a fleet of 1973 Tube Stock trains built by Metro-Cammell of Birmingham (see page 60). Trains are formed of 6-cars which are made up of two 3-car units. Trains are manually driven and the line is signalled with colour lights protected by train stops.

There are a number of service patterns that operate over the Piccadilly which has a mix of end to end workings and a number of shorter workings. On the Heathrow branch, most trains work through to either Heathrow Terminal 5 via Heathrow Terminals 2 & 3, or they go to Heathrow Terminal 4 and call at Heathrow Terminals 2 & 3 on their way back to Central London. There are also trains scheduled to terminate at Northfields and reverse in Northfields Depot. On the Uxbridge branch, some trains terminate at Rayners Lane and head back eastwards via the centre reversing siding at the west end of the station, while some trains continue through to Uxbridge. It is also possible for Piccadilly trains to reverse at Ruislip using the siding that engineering trains use when leaving Ruislip Depot, although Piccadilly Line trains only tend to reverse here at times of disruption. In the eastbound direction, trains can be reversed at Acton Town using one of three sidings (21-23) to the east of the station, and several trains do reverse here at the start and end of traffic in order to get them to or from Northfields depot. The bulk of eastbound trains run through to Cockfosters, but there are a number of short workings which terminate at Arnos Grove. Trains which enter or leave service via the west end of Cockfosters Depot start or finish their journeys at Oakwood. The bulk of these are at the start and end of traffic, but there are a number of trains which do this during the day. At the start of traffic, several trains are booked to enter service towards Heathrow via the west end of Northfields Depot and these enter passenger service at Osterley. Trains that stable at South Harrow, either run empty to Rayners Lane, reverse and enter service from there, or enter service at South Harrow. At the end of traffic, they terminate at Rayners Lane and run empty to South Harrow. On a Sunday morning, there are two trains at the start of traffic that are booked to reverse at King's Cross St Pancras. They arrive from the west into platform 6, and then depart

Piccadilly Line

westbound (at 0657 and 0712) using the crossover normally used by engineering trains heading back to Ruislip Depot. Also on a Sunday morning an empty train runs to Hyde Park Corner where it reverses via the crossover to form the 0705 Hyde Park Corner to Rayners Lane. There are a number of other locations where trains can reverse which can be used at times of service disruption. As well as several crossovers, there are centre reversing sidings at Wood Green, Hammersmith and the closed Down Street station. The latter actually has a train booked to reverse there on Monday to Saturday nights, when an empty train from Arnos Grove reverses in there and then forms an 0025 passenger service from Green Park to Oakwood. In the current timetable, the maximum number of trains in service is 78, which occurs in the morning peak on a Monday to Friday.

The Piccadilly is unique as being the only tube line to feature express running. This takes place between Hammersmith and Acton Town, with the Piccadilly running non-stop, while District Line trains call at Ravenscourt Park, Stamford Brook, Turnham Green and Chiswick Park. This section is four tracks wide, and as a rule, the District Line trains run on the two outer tracks (local lines) with the Piccadilly running on the two centre tracks (fast lines), although Piccadilly Line trains can run on the local lines when needed. Piccadilly Line trains do call at Turnham Green at the start and end of traffic in order to provide better connections with District Line services. Trains call from the start of traffic until 0650 Mondays to Saturdays, until 0745 on Sundays and after 2230 every evening. Between Rayners Lane and Uxbridge, the Piccadilly shares tracks with Metropolitan Line services.

Apart from a short section where the Piccadilly climbs to the surface to cross over the River Crane, the Heathrow branch is entirely in tunnel west of Hounslow West station (partly tube tunnel and partly cut and cover tunnel). Travelling eastbound, the Piccadilly enters tube tunnel to the east of Barons Court station, and emerges into daylight again between Bounds Green and Arnos Grove. There is one further section of tube tunnel which lasts for a distance of roughly half a mile through Southgate.

First trains:

0509 Cockfosters to Heathrow Terminal 5 0640 (Mon-Sat)
0650 Cockfosters to Heathrow Terminal 5 0821 (Sun)
0518 Boston Manor to Cockfosters 0629 (Mon-Sat)*
0620 Heathrow Terminal 4 to Cockfosters 0753 (Sun)

Last trains:

2354 Cockfosters to Heathrow Terminals 2 & 3 0121 (Mon-Sat)
2300 Cockfosters to Heathrow Terminals 2 & 3 0026 (Sun)
2342 Heathrow Terminal 5 to Cockfosters 0114 (Mon-Sat)
2325 Heathrow Terminal 5 to Cockfosters 0056 (Sun)

Note: *The above trains are the first and last trains to travel through the core central section of the line through Central London. There are other shorter workings before and after those listed above.*
This train exits Northfields Depot at the west end and uses the crossover to gain the eastbound line.

A Cockfosters bound Piccadilly Line train passes non-stop through Chiswick Park while passengers wait for the next eastbound District Line service to call. The train is led by unit 199-599-399. 12 December 2015.

VICTORIA LINE →

Victoria Line

Overview:

Route: Walthamstow Central to Brixton.

Route type: Tube

First section opened: Walthamstow Central to Highbury & Islington opened by London Transport on 1 September 1968.

Method of train operation: automatic

Signalling: Invensys Distance to Go (Radio)

Direction of route: Northbound / Southbound.

Route length: 13.3 miles

Number of stations: 16

Trains: 2009 Tube Stock

Max number of trains required (peak times): 39

Depot: Northumberland Park

Stabling points: Walthamstow Central / Brixton / Victoria

HISTORY

The Victoria Line was built by London Transport to relieve congestion on other lines in Central London. Initially it was to be from Walthamstow Central to Victoria, but an extension southwards to Brixton was later authorised. Construction began in 1962, and the first section to open was between Walthamstow Central and Highbury & Islington which opened to passengers on 1 September 1968. The next section to Warren Street opened on 1 December, and then the entire line to Victoria was opened by HM Queen Elizabeth II on 7 March 1969. The extension to Brixton was opened on 23 July 1971, although one station on this section, at Pimlico, did not open until 14 September 1972. The Victoria Line was the first underground railway in the world to feature automatic operation, and it has been operated automatically since opening. The first trains were 1967 Tube Stock trains which operated automatically by receiving codes from the track. These trains were replaced in 2011 by the current trains of 2009 Tube Stock and the signalling system was upgraded.

THE ROUTE AND OPERATIONS

The Victoria Line is worked by a fleet of 2009 Stock built by Bombardier in Derby (see page 69). Trains operate in automatic mode using the Invensys DTG-R system (see page 8). A maximum of 39 trains are required for service, and this maximum is reached in both the

---

Stations (north to south):
- WALTHAMSTOW CENTRAL
- BLACKHORSE ROAD
- TOTTENHAM HALE (Northumberland Park Depot)
- SEVEN SISTERS
- FINSBURY PARK
- *Connection with Piccadilly Line (engineering trains only)*
- HIGHBURY & ISLINGTON
- KING'S CROSS ST. PANCRAS
- EUSTON
- WARREN STREET
- OXFORD CIRCUS
- GREEN PARK
- VICTORIA
- PIMLICO
- VAUXHALL
- STOCKWELL
- BRIXTON

Victoria Line

morning and evening peaks. Most services operate between Brixton and Walthamstow Central, but there are a number of shorter workings from Brixton that terminate at Seven Sisters. Some of these reverse just outside the station on the tracks leading to and from Northumberland Park Depot, while some continue on to Northumberland Park Depot as a staff service. Trains coming from Northumberland Park Depot as a staff service, become a public service upon reaching Seven Sisters. The depot is the only part of the Victoria Line to be out in the open, with the rest of the line being in tube tunnel.

Northumberland Park Depot is the Victoria Line's only depot and the bulk of the fleet stable there outside of traffic hours. A small number of trains stable at other locations as follows: Walthamstow Central (2 trains), Victoria Siding (1 train) and Brixton (3 trains). Centre reversing sidings exist at King's Cross St Pancras (single siding) and Victoria (2 sidings). The King's Cross St Pancras siding is normally only used at times of disruption, although there is a train booked to reverse in there close to the end of traffic on a Sunday. The Victoria Siding has two trains booked to go in there towards the close of traffic each day, one of which reverses, while the other stables.

First trains:
0526 Brixton to Walthamstow Central 0559 (Mon-Sat)
0652 Brixton to Walthamstow Central 0723 (Sun)
0525 Walthamstow Central to Brixton 0557 (Mon-Sat)
0700 Walthamstow Central to Brixton 0733 (Sun)

Last trains:
0028 Brixton to Walthamstow Central 0102 (Mon-Sat)
2352 Brixton to Walthamstow Central 0024 (Sun)
0009 Walthamstow Central to Brixton 0049 (Mon-Sat)
2329 Walthamstow Central to Brixton 0003 (Sun)

Note: The above trains are the first and last trains to travel the entire length of the line. There are other shorter workings before and after those listed above.

A Brixton bound train led by 11055 arrives at Euston on 27 December 2015. Most of the Victoria Line stations were built to a similar design. Each station has its own individual tiled motif in the seat recesses, as seen on the left of this photograph. The Euston motif represents the Doric arch that used to stand at the entrance to Euston mainline station.

Waterloo & City Line

BANK

Overview:

Route: Waterloo to Bank.

Route type: Tube

First section opened: Waterloo to Bank (then called City), opened by the Waterloo & City Railway Company on 8 August 1898.

Method of train operation: Manually driven

Signalling: Colour light signals protected by train stops

Direction of route: Eastbound / westbound.

Route length: 1.5miles

WATERLOO

Number of stations: 2

Trains: 1992 Tube Stock

Max number of trains required (peak times): 5

Waterloo Depot

Depot: Waterloo

Stabling point: Bank

HISTORY

The Waterloo & City Railway was formerly opened by the Duke of Cambridge on 11 July 1898. There was then a slight delay before the line opened to the public on 8 August 1898. The line was built to connect the London & South Western Railway's Waterloo terminus with the City of London. Although the Waterloo & City Railway was operated from the outset by the L&SWR, it was not fully absorbed by them until the first day of 1907. Ownership passed to the Southern Railway (along with the rest of the L&SWR) in 1923, and then, when the railways were nationalised in 1948, to British Rail. The line remained a part of BR (latterly under BR's Network South East banner) until 1994 when it was sold to London Underground. It was also converted from the Southern's third rail system to the London Underground four rail system to coincide with the introduction of new class 482 trains (1992 Stock) towards the end of BR's ownership of the line. It is worth noting that at both Waterloo and Bank, the old Network Southeast logos can still be seen beneath the yellow line near the edges of the platforms.

When opened, what we now know as the Bank terminus of the line was called City. This gave the railway the unusual distinction of having every station name included in its title. The City terminus had been connected below ground by passenger subways with the City & South London Railway (Northern Line) and the Central London Railway (Central Line) at Bank since those lines had opened, but it was not renamed to Bank until October 1940.

The fact that the Waterloo & City was a part of BR until 1994 is reflected in the lack of a physical connection with the rest of the Underground network. Until the building of the now disused Eurostar terminal at Waterloo, W&C trains had to leave the line for maintenance via a lift alongside Waterloo station. The Eurostar terminal was built over the site of the lift, and since its construction, any train needing to leave the W&C has to be craned out.

THE ROUTE AND OPERATIONS

The line is operated by trains of 1992 Tube Stock (see page 62), similar to those operating on the Central Line, but only 4-cars in length. Trains are driven manually in accordance with colour light signals fitted with train stops.

With only two stations, operations are quite straight forward. The depot is situated at the Waterloo

Waterloo & City Line

end of the line beyond the platforms. There are two platforms, number 25 is pick up only and number 26 is set down only. A train entering service will draw forward into platform 25, pick up passengers and then run to Bank. On the approach to Bank, there is a scissors crossover which gives access to the two platforms (numbered 7 and 8). At busy times, at both Waterloo and Bank, the driver of the previous train takes out the next one to reduce the turn round time (known as stepping back). At quieter times, the driver takes out the same train that he brought in. After departing from Bank, trains run directly to platform 26 at Waterloo, which is set down only. Once everybody has detrained, the train will move forward into Waterloo depot to reverse.

The route of the Waterloo & City takes it beneath the Thames just to the west of Blackfriars Bridge. It then turns to the east and runs parallel with the District and Circle lines (albeit at a deeper level) to the terminus at Bank.

The main reason for the existence of this line is to connect the Waterloo mainline terminus with the City of London. There is little need for the railway when the City is quiet. For this reason, the line is closed on Sundays and Bank Holidays.

A maximum of 5 trains are required during the morning and evening peaks on Mondays to Fridays, with 3 trains providing the service outside of the peaks on Mondays to Fridays and all day on Saturday. Train maintenance is carried out at Waterloo, and outside of traffic hours, all bar one train is stabled at Waterloo. One train stables in one of the platforms at Bank.

First trains:
0615 Waterloo to Bank 0620 (Mon-Fri)
0800 Waterloo to Bank 0805 (Sat)
0621 Bank to Waterloo 0626 (Mon-Fri)
0802 Bank to Waterloo 0807 (Sat)

Last trains:
0020 Waterloo to Bank 0025 (Mon-Sat)
0026 Bank to Waterloo 0031 (Mon-Sat)

65510-67510+67509-65509 arrive at Waterloo's platform 26 with a service from Bank on 31 October 2015.

METROPOLITAN LINE →

Metropolitan Line

Overview:

Route: Aldgate to Watford, Uxbridge, Chesham and Amersham.

Route type: Sub-surface

First section opened: Baker Street Junction to Farringdon (opened as part of the Paddington Bishops Road to Farringdon Street line) opened by the Metropolitan Railway on 10 January 1863.

Method of train operation: Manually driven

Signalling: Colour light signals protected by train stops

Direction of route: Northbound / southbound between Baker Street and Amersham, Chesham and Watford plus Harrow to Rayners Lane sub gap), and eastbound / westbound between Aldgate and Baker Street Junction and between Rayners Lane sub gap and Uxbridge.

Route length: 41.5miles

Number of stations: 34

Trains: S Stock (8-car)

Max number of trains required (peak times): 50

Depot: Neasden

Stabling points: Rickmansworth / Watford / Uxbridge

HISTORY

The Metropolitan Railway opened the world's first underground railway on 10 January 1863, which ran between Paddington Bishops Road and Farringdon Street. Today's Metropolitan Line runs over part of that original route from Baker Street Junction to Farringdon. An extension eastwards to Moorgate Street (now Moorgate) was opened on 23 December 1865. The Metropolitan & St John's Wood Railway opened a single track line to Swiss Cottage on 13 April 1868 which diverged from the MR's existing line at Baker Street, forming what we today know as Baker Street Junction. Back at the east end of the MR's line, an extension to the Liverpool Street terminus of the Great Eastern Railway opened on 1 February 1875. This was a temporary arrangement, and the Metropolitan Railway opened the present day Liverpool Street sub-surface station (then called Bishopsgate) on 12 July of the same year. The next extension to Aldgate, the current City terminus of the

Metropolitan Line

Metropolitan Line, opened on 18 November 1876. There was further extension beyond Aldgate, but that is best told as part of the history of the Circle Line, while this chapter concentrates on the sections of railway that make up today's Metropolitan Line.

Extension of the Metropolitan & St John's Wood Railway from Swiss Cottage to West Hampstead opened on 30 June 1879, followed by further extensions to Willesden Green from 24 November 1879, and Harrow-on-the-Hill (then just called Harrow) from 2 August 1880. In 1882, ownership of the Metropolitan & St John's Wood Railway passed to the Metropolitan Railway, and the single track tunnel section north of Baker Street was doubled to increase capacity. The Metropolitan Railway saw itself as a mainline railway and pushed itself further and further away from the capital. On 25 May 1885, an extension north of Harrow to Pinner opened, followed by Rickmansworth on 1 September 1887, and then to a terminus at Chesham which opened on 8 July 1889.

An Aldgate to Chesham service led by 21104 arrives at Pinner on 24 October 2015.

In 1891, the Metropolitan Railway absorbed the Aylesbury & Buckingham Railway, and on 1 September 1892, a line between Chalfont Road (now Chalfont & Latimer) and Aylesbury South Junction was opened, followed in 1894 by a section from Aylesbury South Junction to Aylesbury North Junction which allowed MR trains to run through to Verney Junction, some 50 miles from London. In 1899, the MR took over the Brill branch which diverged from the MR's line at Quainton Road.

On 4 July 1904, the MR opened its line from Harrow-on-the-Hill to Uxbridge, initially with just one intermediate station at Ruislip. The branch to Watford was opened on 2 November 1925, diverging from the MR's main line to the north of Moor Park (then called Moor Park & Sandy Lodge). This was followed in 1932 by the Stanmore branch which opened on 10 December 1932. The Metropolitan Railway became part of London Transport in 1933, and this was followed by a period of contraction as the Brill branch closed in 1935, and Metropolitan trains ceased to run beyond Aylesbury to Verney Junction after July 1936.

With trains coming into London from Aylesbury, Chesham, Watford, Uxbridge and Stanmore, the two track tunnel section north of Baker Street became very congested. As part of the '1935-1940

35

Metropolitan Line

New Works Programme', a new tube tunnel section was built parallel to the Baker Street to Finchley Road section of the Metropolitan, albeit at a deeper level. This surfaced alongside the Metropolitan at Finchley Road. The new tube tunnel section connected with the Bakerloo Line via a new junction at Baker Street, and this section, together with the Stanmore branch were operated by the Bakerloo from 20 November 1939, at which point the Metropolitan ceased to serve Stanmore. The opening of this new section of tube tunnel also resulted in the closure of three stations on the Metropolitan between Baker Street and Finchley Road, these being Lords, Marlborough Road and Swiss Cottage, which were replaced by the new tube stations at St John's Wood and Swiss Cottage.

The Metropolitan Railway had started out dependent on steam traction. Electrification was to follow, but for many years, this only went as far as Rickmansworth, where steam traction would take over on services travelling through to Chesham or Aylesbury. The line north of Rickmansworth was eventually electrified, but only as far as Amersham and Chesham and stations beyond Amersham were served only by British Railways after 9 September 1961. This left the Metropolitan Line as we find it today. There will be further change to the line in the future, as a new chord is being built which will allow Watford trains to run to Watford Junction. This will see the closure of the current Watford Met station, which is likely to be reduced to a train stabling point. This work is not likely to be completed until 2020.

THE ROUTE AND OPERATIONS

The line is worked by a fleet of 8-car S Stock trains built by Bombardier in Derby. Most are purpose built 8-car trains (known as type S8), but at the time of writing, there were two trains formed of a 7-car set (known as type S7), into which an additional car has been inserted from another S7 set. This makes them up to 8-car trains, but they are known as type S7+1 to make them easily distinguished from the S8 sets, as the S7+1 trains have a different internal layout and some slight technical differences. More details about the S Stock can be found on page 53.

The Metropolitan is signalled throughout with colour light signals protected by train stops, although work will be continuing throughout 2016 on installing a new signalling system that will eventually facilitate automatic operation. This will not become live during 2016, and trains will continue to be driven manually for the time being. A maximum of 50 trains are required for service during the evening peak.

The Metropolitan's main depot is at Neasden where all heavy maintenance is carried out. The majority of trains are stabled here outside of traffic hours, but there are also additional stabling points at Watford, Rickmansworth and Uxbridge.

At the London end of the route, trains usually terminate at either Baker Street or Aldgate. Those trains that run through to Aldgate supplement the Circle and Hammersmith & City line services over the north side of the inner circle. From London, trains run to either Watford, Chesham, Amersham or Uxbridge. There are some shorter workings at the start and end of traffic that see trains terminating at Rickmansworth, Harrow-on-the-Hill and Wembley Park. The Metropolitan has always been known for its fast and semi fast services, and while there are fewer of these nowadays, peak hours see a number of trains run fast or semi fast southbound in the morning, and northbound in the evening. Northwards from Wembley Park, the Met has four tracks which are northbound fast / northbound local / southbound local / southbound fast. The fast lines allow the stations at Preston Road and Northwick Park to be missed out. Some trains also pass straight through Wembley Park, but there are platforms on the fast lines here, and some trains do call at these platforms. Harrow-on-the-Hill is a major hub on the Metropolitan and is where the Uxbridge branch diverges. There is also interchange here with Network Rail services operated by Chiltern Railways, which have been running alongside the Metropolitan since Finchley Road. North of Harrow-on-the-Hill, towards Watford, Amersham and Chesham, there are once again four tracks which are divided up as northbound main / southbound main / northbound local / southbound local. The Chiltern Railways services share the northbound and southbound main with the Metropolitan, and these two tracks

Metropolitan Line

miss out the stations at North Harrow, Pinner, Northwood Hills and Northwood which are only served by trains running on the local lines.

North of Moor Park at Watford South Junction, trains can either go straight on towards Rickmansworth, Chesham and Amersham, or go right towards Watford. This is part of a triangular junction, the North Curve of which is mainly used by empty stock workings. However, there are a number of trains that traverse this curve in passenger service as follows:

0515 Chesham to Watford (Mon to Sat)

0049 Watford to Rickmansworth (Mon to Fri)*

0700 Rickmansworth to Watford (Sun)

0029 Watford to Rickmansworth (Sun)*

*These trains are at the end of traffic of the days denoted, for example the 0029 shown as Sunday is at the end of Sunday's traffic, although technically, it is Monday by the time the train runs – just to avoid any potential confusion.

First trains:
0520 Baker Street to Uxbridge 0602 (Mon-Sat)
0658 Baker Street to Uxbridge 0738 (Sun)
0511 Uxbridge to Aldgate 0609 (Mon-Sat)
0635 Uxbridge to Aldgate 0735 (Sun)

Last trains:
0043 Baker Street to Uxbridge 0123 (Mon-Sat)
2359 Aldgate to Uxbridge 0100 (Sun)
0003 Uxbridge to Baker Street 0043 (Mon-Sat)
2328 Chesham to Baker Street 0025 (Sun)

Note: *The above trains are the first and last trains to serve the Central London stations at either Baker Street or Aldgate and the extremities of one of the Metropolitan's branches. There are other shorter workings before and after those listed above.*

An Aldgate to Uxbridge Metropolitan Line service led by 21036 arrives at a very quiet Great Portland Street station on 21 June 2015. This section of line is served by trains on the Metropolitan, Hammersmith & City and Circle lines and is one of the busiest stretches of line on the Underground system with up to 30 trains per hour, matched by the southern part of the District and beaten only by the Central Line (westbound morning peaks) and the Victoria Line.

HAMMERSMITH & CITY LINE →

Hammersmith & City Line

Overview:

Route: Hammersmith to Barking

Route type: Sub-surface

First section opened: Paddington Bishops Road to Farringdon Street opened by the Metropolitan Railway on 10 January 1863.

Method of train operation: Manually driven

Signalling: Colour light signals protected by train stops

Direction of route: Eastbound / westbound.

Route length: 16 miles

Number of stations: 29

Trains: S Stock (7-car)

Max number of trains required (peak times): 33 (combined with Circle Line services)

Depots: Neasden / Ealing Common / Upminster (see notes in 'The Route and Operations')

Stabling points: Hammersmith / Barking / Upminster / Wembley Park / Aldgate / Edgware Road / Triangle Sidings

HISTORY

The Hammersmith & City Line operates over the Hammersmith branch, the northern side of the inner circle and along former Metropolitan District Railway lines to Barking, and so shares its history with those lines. The middle section of the Hammersmith & City includes the world's oldest underground railway which was opened by the Metropolitan Railway between Paddington Bishops Road and Farringdon Street on 10 January 1863. The Hammersmith branch was opened as a joint venture between the MR and the Great Western Railway, and this opened from Paddington to Hammersmith on 13 June 1864. Initially operated by the GWR, a year after opening MR took over services to Hammersmith while the GWR operated trains to Addison Road (now Kensington Olympia) which was reached via a junction at Latimer Road. This service was suspended in October 1940 due to bomb damage, but never resumed.

In 1869, the London & South Western Railway opened a line from Addison Road to Richmond which came alongside the Hammersmith terminus and had its own station called Grove Road. A link was built between the H&C and the L&SWR's line to the north of Hammersmith station (known as Grove Road Junction), and some trains ran onto the L&SWR from the H&C. This connection was taken out of service in 1916 along with the station at Hammersmith Grove Road. Traces of the former junction can still be seen to the north of Hammersmith station.

At the east end of what now forms the Hammersmith & City Line, the Metropolitan Railway had extended beyond

---

- HAMMERSMITH
- GOLDHAWK ROAD
- SHEPHERD'S BUSH MARKET
- WOOD LANE
- LATIMER ROAD
- LADBROKE GROVE
- WESTBOURNE PARK
- ROYAL OAK
- PADDINGTON
- EDGWARE ROAD
- BAKER STREET
- GREAT PORTLAND STREET
- EUSTON SQUARE
- KING'S CROSS ST. PANCRAS
- FARRINGDON
- BARBICAN
- MOORGATE
- LIVERPOOL STREET
- ALDGATE EAST
- WHITECHAPEL
- STEPNEY GREEN
- MILE END
- BOW ROAD
- BROMLEY-BY-BOW
- WEST HAM
- PLAISTOW
- UPTON PARK
- EAST HAM
- BARKING

Hammersmith & City Line

Farringdon Street to Aldgate and then in 1884, MR trains were extended via a curve to Aldgate East where they joined the tracks of the Metropolitan District Railway to St Mary's near Whitechapel. Here they turned off the MDR tracks and joined the East London Railway (now part of the London Overground network) and worked through to New Cross. From 1936, some Hammersmith trains were scheduled to run to Barking instead of the ELR, and then Hammersmith trains ceased running to and from the ELR in 1939.

Until 1990, what we today know as the Hammersmith & City Line was shown on the Underground map as a part of the Metropolitan Line. From 1990, the line gained its own identity as the Hammersmith & City Line denoted by the colour pink on the Underground map. The Hammersmith branch was served exclusively by Hammersmith & City Line trains until December 2009, at which point Circle Line services (running Hammersmith – Edgware Road – Victoria – Edgware Road and vice versa) also ran onto the Hammersmith branch in order to increase the frequency of service.

THE ROUTE AND OPERATIONS

The Hammersmith & City Line is operated by 7-car trains of S Stock (S7) built by Bombardier of Derby. The S7 fleet operate across the Circle, Hammersmith & City and District lines, and there is no dedicated fleet specifically for the Hammersmith & City Line. Therefore the H&C's trains are maintained at the depots tasked with the job of maintaining the S7 fleet, which are Ealing Common and Upminster on the District Line, and Neasden on the Metropolitan Line. Hammersmith depot is now a stabling point at which trains being used on the Circle and Hammersmith & City lines stable outside of traffic hours. Trains also stable in Barking sidings at the east end of the route. A number of trains also stable in Wembley Park Sidings which are only long enough to accommodate S7s and cannot accommodate the longer S8s that operate on the adjacent Metropolitan Line. Trains stabling in Wembley Park sidings run empty from Baker Street to Harrow-on-the-Hill where they reverse in order to reach Wembley Park sidings. In the opposite direction, trains run empty directly from Wembley Park sidings to Baker Street. Close to the end of traffic, there are a number of trains which run to Upminster Depot to stable. This gives the unusual sight of trains leaving Hammersmith with Upminster as a destination as they carry passengers all the way to Upminster station. The reverse of this happens in the morning, when they leave Upminster Depot and enter passenger service at Upminster station with Hammersmith as their destination. Plaistow used to be a common reversing point for H&C trains, but today sees only a small number which reverse here close to the end of traffic or during times of disruption.

With the exception of Subway Tunnel, the Hammersmith branch is all above ground. From Hammersmith to Westbourne Park, the line runs on top of brick viaducts giving passengers a pleasant view down on to the colourful Shepherd's Bush Market and the former BBC Television studios at Wood Lane. At Westbourne Park, the line comes alongside the Network Rail tracks of the Great Western Main Line just outside of the Paddington terminus. The Underground tracks dive down into Subway Tunnel, which takes them beneath the Network Rail tracks between Westbourne Park and Royal Oak. The line then runs parallel to Paddington main line terminus and serves platforms 15 and 16. East of Paddington, H&C trains are joined by the Circle and District lines from High Street Kensington at Praed Street Junction, and then run around the top of the inner circle as far as Aldgate Junction where they branch to the left and then join the District Line at Aldgate East. From here, the tracks are shared between the Hammersmith & City and District lines all the way through to the end of the Hammersmith & City Line at Barking. The District does, however, continue beyond Barking to Upminster.

The maximum number of trains required for service is 33, which occurs in both the morning and evening peaks. This figure is slightly misleading however, as it also includes Circle Line trains, as the two lines are jointly managed.

Hammersmith & City Line

First trains:
0457 Hammersmith to Barking 0555 (Mon-Sat)
0707 Hammersmith to Barking 0806 (Sun)
0501 Barking to Hammersmith 0559 (Mon-Sat)
0626 Barking to Hammersmith 0725 (Sun)

Last trains:
0014 Hammersmith to Barking 0111 (Mon-Sat)
2354 Hammersmith to Barking 0055 (Sun)
2335 Barking to Hammersmith 0034 (Mon-Sat)
2315 Barking to Hammersmith 0014 (Sun)

Note: The above trains are the first and last trains to serve the entire length of the line. There are other shorter workings before and after those listed above.

A Hammersmith to Barking service arrives at Barking led by 21301 on 7 March 2015.

CIRCLE LINE →

Circle Line

Overview:

Route: Hammersmith to Edgware Road, then via King's Cross St Pancras, Aldgate, Tower Hill, Victoria, High Street Kensington and Notting Hill Gate to Edgware Road

Route type: Sub-surface

First section opened: Paddington Bishops Road to Farringdon Street opened by the Metropolitan Railway on 10 January 1863.

Method of train operation: Manually driven

Signalling: Colour light signals protected by train stops

Direction of route: Outer rail (clockwise) / Inner rail (counter-clockwise) and eastbound / westbound on the Hammersmith branch.

Route length: 17 miles

Number of stations: 36

Trains: S Stock (7-car)

Max number of trains required (peak times): 33 (combined with Hammersmith & City Line services)

Depots: Neasden / Ealing Common / Upminster (see notes in 'The Route and Operations')

Stabling points: Hammersmith / Edgware Road / Barking / Moorgate / Triangle Sidings / Wembley Park / Upminster

HISTORY

The history of the Circle Line, like the Hammersmith & City and the Metropolitan, starts with the world's first underground railway opened by the Metropolitan Railway between Paddington Bishops Road and Farringdon Street on 10 January 1863. As the underground railways of London developed, a select committee recommended the linking together of underground lines to form an 'inner circle' around London that would link the London termini of the mainline railway companies. The London

Circle Line

termini are all on the outskirts of Central London, as the mainline railway companies had been prevented from building their lines into the heart of the city. In 1868, the Metropolitan Railway built a line that diverged from its existing line at Praed Street Junction (between Edgware Road and Paddington), that passed through Bayswater and Notting Hill Gate to Gloucester Road (then called Brompton Gloucester Road) which opened on 1 October 1868. This was then extended to South Kensington, where it met a new railway in the form of the Metropolitan District Railway's South Kensington to Westminster Bridge (now Westminster) line. Both the MR's short extension and the MDR's line opened for business on the same day, 24 December 1868. The MDR extended eastwards, opening to Blackfriars on 30 May 1870, and then to Mansion House on 3 July 1871. The underground railways now formed a big 'C' around the capital, and when the MR extended to Liverpool Street and then Aldgate (18 November 1876), the 'inner circle' was almost complete except for a gap between Mansion House and Aldgate.

The similarity in names between the Metropolitan Railway and the Metropolitan District Railway was no coincidence, as it had been the intention that the two companies would eventually merge. Instead they became bitter rivals with a reluctance to complete the 'inner circle'. It eventually took an Act of Parliament to force them to do so.

On 25 September 1882, the MR extended to a station called Tower of London, which was on the site of the current Tower Hill station. The MDR extended eastwards to Whitechapel, and this line opened on 6 October 1884. Part of this line completed the 'inner circle'. The MR's Tower of London station was closed on 12 October 1884, and a new station called Mark Lane was opened in its place just a short distance to the west. The clockwise service was operated by the MR, with a mix of MR and MDR trains operating the anti-clockwise service.

This is a very brief description of how the 'inner circle' came to be, but the construction, arguments and operating arrangements of this railway could fill a book on their own.

Although the 'inner circle' was completed in 1884, the Circle Line did not appear as a separate colour on the Underground map until 1949. It operated as a complete circle until 13 December 2009 when the Hammersmith branch was incorporated in order to increase train frequencies on that branch.

THE ROUTE AND OPERATIONS

The Circle Line is operated by 7-car S Stock trains (S7). The S7 fleet operate across the Circle, Hammersmith & City and District lines; there is no dedicated fleet specifically for the Circle Line, therefore the Circle's trains are maintained at the depots tasked with the job of maintaining the S7 fleet, which are Ealing Common and Upminster on the District Line, and Neasden on the Metropolitan Line. Circle Line train operation is managed jointly with the Hammersmith & City Line, and the maximum requirement for trains across both lines is 33, which occurs in both the morning and evening peaks.

Since 13 December 2009, the Circle Line no longer just goes round in a circle. From that date, the Circle Line has included the Hammersmith branch, making it better resemble a tea cup than a circle. The reason the Hammersmith branch was added was to increase the service frequency on that line. Today, trains start from Hammersmith and run to Edgware Road (usually platform 1). They then run around the outer rail through King's Cross St Pancras, Aldgate, Tower Hill, Victoria and High Street Kensington to Edgware Road, where they terminate (usually in platform 2). They then head back all the way around the inner rail, then pass through Edgware Road (usually through platform 4) and then run to Hammersmith to terminate there. At the start and end of each day, there are some variations in the workings in order to get trains to the various stabling points. Perhaps the most unusual of which is on a Saturday night when the 2251 from Hammersmith goes around the outer rail, and then instead of terminating at Edgware Road, carries on around the top of the 'inner circle' and then becomes a service for Upminster, where it terminates and proceeds into Upminster Depot.

A Circle Line train spends most of its journey sharing tracks with other lines. The Hammersmith branch and the top of the 'inner circle' are shared with the Hammersmith & City Line, and also the

Circle Line

A Circle Line train for Hammersmith arrives at Farringdon on 31 October 2015. The train is proudly displaying a poppy on the front, something that London Underground does each year in honour of Remembrance Day.

Circle Line

Metropolitan Line from Baker Street Junction to Aldgate. The south side of the 'inner circle' from Minories Junction (between Aldgate and Tower Hill) to Gloucester Road is shared with the District Line, and from High Street Kensington to Edgware Road is also shared with the District. There are just two locations where the Circle has exclusive use of the tracks. The first is through Aldgate to Minories Junction. The Hammersmith & City turns away towards Aldgate East to the north of Aldgate station, and although the Metropolitan Line serves Aldgate, it uses the two middle platforms (2 and 3), while only the Circle uses the outer platforms (1 and 4) and the short section of line between Aldgate station and Minories Junction where the District joins. The second location is the curve between Gloucester Road and High Street Kensington.

First trains:
0448 Hammersmith to Edgware Road 0603 (Mon-Sat)
0621 Hammersmith to Edgware Road 0734 (Sun)
0528 Edgware Road to Hammersmith 0639 (Mon-Sat)
0707 Edgware Road to Hammersmith 0819 (Sun)

Last trains:
2331 Hammersmith to Edgware Road 0042 (Mon-Sat)
2311 Hammersmith to Edgware Road 0022 (Sun)
2350 Edgware Road to Hammersmith 0059 (Mon-Sat)
2330 Edgware Road to Hammersmith 0039 (Sun)

Note: The above trains are the first and last trains to serve the entire Hammersmith branch and complete circuit of the 'inner circle'. There are other shorter workings before and after those listed above.

21404 is seen in one of the bay platforms (number 3) at Moorgate with a short working Circle Line service. The short working had been due to an operational issue earlier in the day. 31 October 2014.

DISTRICT LINE →

RICHMOND
KEW GARDENS
GUNNERSBURY

WIMBLEDON
WIMBLEDON PARK
SOUTHFIELDS
EAST PUTNEY
PUTNEY BRIDGE
PARSONS GREEN

FULHAM BROADWAY
WEST BROMPTON

GLOUCESTER ROAD
SOUTH KENSINGTON
SLOANE SQUARE
VICTORIA
ST JAMES'S PARK
WESTMINSTER
EMBANKMENT
TEMPLE
BLACKFRIARS
MANSION HOUSE
CANNON STREET
MONUMENT
TOWER HILL
ALDGATE EAST
WHITECHAPEL
STEPNEY GREEN
MILE END
BOW ROAD
BROMLEY-BY-BOW
WEST HAM
PLAISTOW
UPTON PARK
EAST HAM
BARKING
UPNEY
BECONTREE
DAGENHAM HEATHWAY
DAGENHAM EAST
ELM PARK
HORNCHURCH
UPMINSTER BRIDGE
UPMINSTER

Upminster Depot

EALING BROADWAY
EALING COMMON

Ealing Common Depot

ACTON TOWN
CHISWICK PARK
TURNHAM GREEN
STAMFORD BROOK
RAVENSCOURT PARK
HAMMERSMITH
BARONS COURT
WEST KENSINGTON

EARL'S COURT
KENSINGTON (OLYMPIA)

HIGH STREET KENSINGTON
NOTTING HILL GATE
BAYSWATER
PADDINGTON
EDGWARE ROAD

District Line

Overview:

Route: Upminster to Ealing Broadway with branches to Richmond, Wimbledon, Kensington (Olympia), High Street Kensington and Edgware Road

Route type: Sub-surface

First section opened: South Kensington to Westminster Bridge opened by the Metropolitan District Railway on 24 December 1868.

Method of train operation: Manually driven

Signalling: Colour light signals protected by train stops

Direction of route: Eastbound / westbound.

Route length: 40 miles

Number of stations: 60

Trains: S Stock (7-car) / D Stock (6-car)

Max number of trains required (peak times): 76

Depots: Upminster and Ealing Common

Stabling points: Lillie Bridge / Parsons Green / Barking / Triangle Sidings / Richmond / High Street Kensington

HISTORY

The Metropolitan District Railway opened a line from South Kensington to Westminster (then called Westminster Bridge) on 24 December 1868. An extension westwards to West Brompton opened on 12 April 1869, and this was followed by two extensions at the east end, first to Blackfriars on 30 May 1870, and then to Mansion House on 3 July 1871, the same day as a short spur off of the West Brompton line from Earl's Court round to High Street Kensington was also opened. Another line to branch off the West Brompton line took the MDR to West Kensington, and this opened on 1 February 1872. A further spur off of this line opened on the same day and allowed trains to run through to Addison Road (now Kensington Olympia). The West Kensington branch was further extended to Hammersmith, and this opened on 9 September 1874. On 1 June 1877, a short link was opened from the MDR at Hammersmith to the London & South Western Railway's line, the two lines coming together at Studland Road Junction, which allowed MDR trains to run through to Richmond. The MDR then built a line to Ealing Broadway which branched off of the L&SWR's line at Turnham Green. This opened on 1 July 1879. The West Brompton branch was extended as far as the River Thames, opening to Putney Bridge & Fulham (now just called Putney Bridge) on 1 March 1880. A branch to Hounslow was built which diverged from

District Line

The D Stock has formed the backbone of the District Line fleet since 1980, but will soon be replaced by the S Stock fleet. In this view, unit 7088-17088-8088 (which has been withdrawn from service since this photograph was taken) is seen departing from Upney with a service for Upminster on 1 March 2015. Upney is on the section of line between Barking and Upminster where the LMS added two tracks for District services in 1932. The two District tracks are on the left, with the former LT&SR mainline tracks to and from Shoeburyness and Southend on the right.

the Ealing Broadway branch at Acton Town (then called Mill Hill Park), opening to Hounslow Town on 1 May 1883, and then a line which by-passed Hounslow Town was opened to Hounslow Barracks on 21 July 1884. This left Hounslow Town as a terminus on a short branch, which then closed on 31 March 1886.

At the east end of the District, the line was extended from Mansion House to Whitechapel on 6 October 1884. This opening saw the completion of the 'inner circle' with the Metropolitan Railway. From March 1883 to September 1885, the District Railway (as the MDR had become more commonly known by then), operated trains through to Windsor running over Great Western Railway tracks beyond Ealing Broadway.

The L&SWR opened a line from Wimbledon and built the Fulham Rail Bridge over the River Thames which allowed them to join up with the District Railway's Putney Bridge & Fulham branch. The District had running powers over this line, and the first District train ran through to Wimbledon on 3 June 1889.

The District began operating to East Ham from 2 June 1902 following the construction of a link between it and the London, Tilbury & Southend Railway. Some trains also continued along the LT&SR to Upminster until 30 September 1905. At the west end of the District, a very short branch was opened on 13 June 1905 from Mill Hill Park to South Acton. The Hounslow Town branch also re-opened, this time with a spur allowing trains to arrive into the terminus from the east, and then depart to the west to Hounslow Barracks. Hounslow Town re-opened on 1 March 1903, but then closed again on 1 May 1909, never to re-open. A line to South Harrow was opened on 28 June 1903. The eventual aim was Uxbridge, and a short extension was opened from South Harrow to Rayners Lane, where the District joined the tracks of the Metropolitan over which it obtained running rights. District trains ran through to Uxbridge from 1 March 1910.

Widening of the track formation at the east end of the line saw District trains segregated from those

District Line

of the LT&SR and electrification through to Barking from July 1908. In 1932, the London Midland & Scottish Railway (successors to the LT&SR) added a new pair of electrified tracks between Barking and Upminster for exclusive use by District trains. This allowed the LMS to speed up their own services with the District trains segregated and making most of the station stops on this stretch of railway.

There then followed a period of contraction as the Acton Town to South Harrow route was taken over by the Piccadilly Line from 4 July 1932, although District trains still operated a shuttle from South Harrow to Uxbridge until the Piccadilly took over that section too from 23 October 1933. In March 1933, the Piccadilly also took over most of the services to Hounslow West (the former Hounslow Barracks station, which had been renamed in 1925), although the District still operated some peak hour services over this route until 1964. The branch from Acton Town to South Acton closed on 28 February 1959, leaving the District Line as we find it today.

THE ROUTE AND OPERATIONS

At the time of compiling this guide book, the District Line was being operated by a mix of D Stock (see page 50) and 7-car S Stock (see page 53). The S Stock will eventually replace the older D Stock, and the end for the D Stock is likely to come towards the end of 2016, or maybe the beginning of 2017. Some of the D Stock is being sold to Viva Rail for conversion to diesel trains and possible future use on Network Rail, while some vehicles are being scrapped. The remaining D Stock is only used on the District Line, but the S7 trains that are replacing them are in a pool fleet that can be used on the District, Hammersmith & City and Circle lines. The D Stock will be the last trains to be replaced by the new S Stock, and once the D Stock has gone from the District, the entire sub-surface railway will be operated by the S Stock trains.

The District Line has more stations than any other Underground line (60), and runs east to west across London. Upminster Depot is the furthest easterly point reached by the entire Underground, while Upminster station is the most easterly point that is reached by Underground trains in

A train of S Stock led by 21422 arrives at Bromley-by-Bow with a District Line service for Dagenham East on 29 August 2015. Since this photograph was taken, the crossover in the distance has been decommissioned and removed.

47

District Line

passenger service. The section from Upminster to Barking is on segregated tracks built by the LMS in 1932. Westwards from Barking, the District shares tracks with Hammersmith & City Line services as far as Aldgate East. Here, the H&C turns right towards Liverpool Street, and the District turns left and joins the Circle Line at Minories Junction. District trains then share tracks with Circle Line trains along the bottom section of the 'inner circle' through Mansion House, Westminster and Victoria to Gloucester Road, where the Circle Line turns towards High Street Kensington. The District carries on to Earl's Court, which is considered to be the hub of the District Line. From here, there are branches to High Street Kensington and Edgware Road, Wimbledon, Richmond and Ealing Broadway.

Train services over the District Line are a mixture of full length workings, together with a number of shorter workings. The bulk of services operate over the full length from Upminster to either Richmond or Ealing Broadway. Shorter workings operate between Wimbledon and Edgware Road, Wimbledon and Tower Hill, Wimbledon and Barking and Kensington (Olympia) and High Street Kensington. This latter service usually only operates at weekends or Bank Holidays or when there is an exhibition taking place at Olympia. There are also a number trains that operate between Wimbledon and Dagenham East during peak hours. The maximum number of trains required for service is 76, which occurs during the evening peaks. An unusual pair of workings operates on a Sunday morning, with the 0537 and 0557 departures from Upminster both scheduled to reverse at Aldgate East via the crossover east of the station.

The line has two main depots at Upminster and Ealing Common. The D Stock is only maintained at these two depots, but the replacement S Stock is in a common user fleet, and so will also receive attention at Neasden when necessary. In addition to the main depots, trains engaged on District Line duties also stable at Richmond, Lillie Bridge, Parsons Green, Triangle Sidings, High Street Kensington and Barking.

First trains:
0453 Upminster to Richmond 0622 (Mon-Sat)
0609 Upminster to Richmond 0738 (Sun)
0451 Ealing Broadway to Upminster 0623 (Mon-Sat)
0617 Ealing Broadway to Upminster 0748 (Sun)

Last trains:
2341 Upminster to Ealing Broadway 0112 (Mon-Sat)
2307 Upminster to Ealing Broadway 0038 (Sun)
0003 Richmond to Upminster 0133 (Mon-Sat)
2329 Richmond to Upminster 0100 (Sun)

Note: *The above trains are the first and last trains to serve the entire length of the District Line. There are other shorter workings before and after those listed above.*

The Trains

D Stock

THE TRAINS

The following section describes each type of train currently in operation on London Underground together with stock lists. The following information and abbreviations apply:

DM – Driving motor (powered vehicle with a driving cab at one end)

NDM – Non-driving motor (powered vehicle with no driving cab)

UNDM – Uncoupling non-driving motor (powered vehicle with no driving cab but fitted with controls at one end to allow uncoupling and shunting)

T – Trailer (vehicle with no motors and no cabs)

M – Non-driving motor car (powered vehicle with no driving cab)

MS – Motor Shoegear (powered vehicle with shoe gear and semi-permanent couplings allowing trains to split for maintenance)

Trains have an 'A' end and a 'D' end. On the Bakerloo, Victoria, Waterloo & City and Jubilee lines, trains always face the same way as there is nowhere on those lines where trains can become turned. Bakerloo trains always have the 'A' car facing south, but on the Victoria, Waterloo & City and Jubilee lines, the 'A' car faces either north or west. This also applies to the D Stock on the District Line, which always have the 'A' car facing west.

With the 7-car S Stock trains working from a pool covering the Hammersmith & City, Circle and District lines, they can become turned depending on what routes they take and where they stable. The 8-car S Stock trains on the Metropolitan Line are turned if they work round the Watford North Curve, and the 1995 Stock trains on the Northern Line are turned each time they go round the Kennington loop. The 1992 Stock on the Central Line is designed to be fully reversible and runs with an 'A' car at both ends. The Hainault loop at the east end of the Central Line is what causes these trains to become turned.

When in service, each train is allocated a three digit reporting number, from which that train's duty can be identified. The number is allocated to the train at the start of its duty and it is displayed on the front and rear of the train. On engineering trains, heritage trains and the D Stock fleet, the reporting number is displayed as numbers on plates that are slotted into a holder in order to display the correct number. On all other trains, the three digit number is displayed digitally either as part of the destination display, or in a separate digital display in the cab window (as per the 1972 Stock). This number is allocated to the train at the start of its duty, and is a way of identifying the train in the working timetable.

D STOCK

Size of stock: Sub-surface
Year of manufacture: 1978-1981
Built by: Metro-Cammell, Birmingham
Entry into service: 1980
Lines used on: District
Number of cars per train: 6
Train formation: DM-T-UNDM+UNDM-T-DM or DM-T-UNDM+DM-T-DM
    or DM-T-DM+UNDM-T-DM or DM-T-DM+DM-T-DM

More commonly known as D Stock, these trains are also sometimes referred to as D78 Stock (1978 being the intended year of manufacture). They have always been associated with the District Line, and can work all routes of the District except for the section north of High Street Kensington, where the trains are too long for the short platforms at Notting Hill Gate, Bayswater and Paddington. District Line trains over this route were worked by the shorter C Stock trains until their withdrawal in 2014, and are now worked by 7-car S Stock trains, which are also too long for these platforms, but their open plan interiors and selective door opening allow passengers to walk through to the nearest available opening door.

D Stock

A Richmond bound train of D Stock led by double ended unit 7514-17514-7515 arrives at Monument on 29 August 2015. The raised strips will be noted on the corners of the cab front. These are the inter-car barrier fixings that distinguish this as a double ended unit. The single ended units do not have these (see next page)

The D Stock operates as 6-car trains which are formed of two 3-car units. Most of these are single ended with a DM at one end and a UNDM at the other, but there are a number of double ended units which have a DM at both ends. Trains can be formed of two single ended units (provided one is a west facing unit and the other is an east facing unit), two double ended units or a single ended unit with a double ended unit. The double ended units can be easily identified from the single ended units as the DMs have inter-car barrier fixings on each cab for use when that cab is formed in the middle of a train.

The D Stock fleet is in the process of being withdrawn, and 2016 could well be their final year in service. They are being replaced by 7-car S Stock trains on all District Line services. This does not spell the end for the D Stock though, as two units have been sent to Acton for conversion into a new Rail Adhesion Train (with two more units expected to follow). It is also expected that a unit or two may be retained for Emergency Response Unit (ERU) training. Most of the withdrawn vehicles are being sold to a company called Viva Rail, which plans to convert them into diesel powered trains for use on Network Rail. Once withdrawn, the vehicles are either sent to Long Marston (for Viva Rail) or to

Single ended unit 7018-17018-8018 leads a westbound train into Plaistow on 7 March 2015.

51

D Stock

D Stock
West Facing Units

DM(A)	T	UNDM	DM(A)	T	UNDM	DM(A)	T	UNDM	DM(A)	T	UNDM
7000	17000	8000	7020	17020	8020	7036	17036	8036	7084	17084	8084
7002	17002	8002	7022	17022	8022	7038	17038	8038	7086	17086	8086
7004	17004	8004	7024	17024	8024	7040	17040	8040	7098	17098	8098
7006	17006	8006	7026	17026	8026	7042	17042	8042	7106	17106	8106
7012	17012	8012	7028	17028	8028	7044	17044	8044	7108	17108	8108
7014	17014	8014	7030	17030	8030	7046	17046	8046	7110	17110	8110
7016	17016	8016	7032	17032	8032	7048	17048	8048			
7018	17018	8018	7034	17034	8034	7070	17070	8070			

East facing Units

UNDM	T	DM(D)	UNDM	T	DM(D)	UNDM	T	DM(D)	UNDM	T	DM(D)
8005	17005	7005	8043	17043	7043	8083	17083	7083	8105	17105	7105
8007	17007	7007	8051	17051	7051	8091	17091	7091	8107	17107	7107
8011	17011	7011	8053	17053	7053	8093	17093	7093	8109	17109	7109
8017	17017	7017	8057	17057	7057	8095	17095	7095	8111	17111	7111
8021	17021	7021	8061	17061	7061	8097	17097	7097	8115	17115	7115
8031	17031	7031	8071	17071	7071	8099	17099	7099	8121	17121	7121
8033	17033	7033	8075	17075	7075	8101	17101	7101	8127	17127	7127
8037	17037	7037	8079	17079	7079	8103	17103	7103			

Double Ended Units

DM(A)	T	DM(D)	DM(A)	T	DM(D)	DM(A)	T	DM(D)	DM(A)	T	DM(D)
7500	17500	7501	7508	17508	7509	7520	17520	7521	7530	17530	7531
7502	17502	7503	7512	17512	7513	7524	17524	7525	7532	17532	7533
7504	17504	7505	7516	17516	7517	7526	17526	7527	7534	17534	7535
7506	17506	7507	7518	17518	7519	7528	17528	7529	7536	17536	7537
									7538	17538	7539

Interior view of a D Stock driving motor showing the mix of longitudinal and transverse seating.

Booth's of Rotherham for scrap. Viva Rail are not taking any of the UNDM vehicles, and these are going for scrap, together with some of the trailers.

A final date for D Stock trains is not certain at the time of going to press and is dependent on deliveries of new S Stock trains. One thing is for sure, there will not be much time left to enjoy these trains in London Underground service.

S STOCK

Size of stock: Sub-surface
Year of manufacture: 2009 onwards
Built by: Bombardier Transportation, Derby
Entry into service: 2010
Lines used on: Metropolitan, Circle, Hammersmith & City and District lines
Number of cars per train: 7 (S7) and 8 (S8 and S7+1)
Train formation: DM-M1-M2-MS-MS-M2-M1-DM (S8 and S7+1)
                         DM-M1-M2-MS-MS-M1-DM (S7)

A Barking to Hammersmith service on the Hammersmith & City Line is seen on Barking flyover with 21360 bringing up the rear. 7 March 2015.

The S Stock is being introduced across the entire sub-surface network. They have already replaced the A Stock on the Metropolitan, the C Stock on the Hammersmith & City, Circle and District lines, and are in the process of replacing the D Stock on the District Line. Once the D Stock has been phased out, the entire sub-surface network will be operated by S Stock trains.

The S Stock is fitted with air conditioning, the first train type on the Underground to have this feature from new (a car was converted as an experiment as long ago as 1935). The trains also have an open plan interior, and rather than individual cars separated by emergency doors as on all other Underground trains, passengers can walk through the interior from one end to the other. This has a number of advantages. The area that would have been occupied by the car ends and the emergency inter-car doors is used as additional standing area, thus increasing capacity, there is greater security for passengers, and it also allows passengers to walk through to the nearest available opening door when they call at stations with short platforms.

The S Stock trains are longer than the trains that they have replaced (or are replacing), and where possible, platforms have been lengthened to accommodate them. There are some places where this has not been possible, the west side of the Circle Line for example, where the retaining walls would have had to be moved in order to lengthen the platforms. Where platforms are shorter than

S Stock

This picture shows an S7 set pulled up at the Hammersmith terminus of the Circle and Hammersmith & City lines. The marker boards with 'S7' displayed on them show the train operator where to pull up in order to be in the right place to open the passenger doors. The driver lines up the area between the chevrons with the edge of the cab window.

the S Stock, they pull up with each end of the train beyond the ends of the platforms. The doors that are not lined up with the platforms do not open, and passengers can walk through to the nearest available opening door. An illuminated 'Door not in use' sign lights up shortly after leaving the previous station, and localised announcements inside the train stating that 'doors will not open here' are repeated several times prior to the train arriving at the station with short platforms.

All S Stock trains are fitted with lighting at floor level by each door which is illuminated whenever the doors are opened as an aid to any passenger with a visual impairment.

S Stock trains pull up at stopping boards which display the following codes, depending on their location and use: S7 = stopping point for 7-car S Stock / S8 = stopping point for 8-car S Stock / SS = stopping point for both 7-car and 8-car S Stock / SR = stopping point for a train of S Stock making a reversing move.

The S Stock trains come in two distinct types, the 8-car S8 and the 7-car S7. The S7 sets are used on the Circle, Hammersmith & City and District lines, and operate from a common pool, meaning that an S7 set can turn up on any of these three lines. The seating inside the S7 sets is all longitudinal, leaving more room for standing passengers. This reflects the fact that they mostly operate on lines where lots of short journeys are made. The S8 sets are dedicated to the Metropolitan Line, and differ internally from the S7s as they have an amount of transverse seating, reflecting the fact that the Metropolitan Line is more of an outer suburban railway, where average journey lengths are longer, and thus extra seating capacity is provided.

There is a third type, known as the S7+1. These are the three S7 sets that have had an extra car added to make them up to 8-cars for use on the Metropolitan Line, initially to cover for S8s that had to return to Derby for engineering modifications. It had been the intention that these sets would all revert to their standard S7 configuration, but it would now appear that the plan is for one train to revert to S7 configuration during 2016, one is to remain as an S7+1 to cover for trains going back to Derby for the fitting of ATC equipment, which will then eventually revert to S7 configuration, and finally, one will remain as an S7+1 and will remain in the Metropolitan Line fleet as an additional

S Stock

train that will be required when the Croxley Link is opened. An additional S7 train is to be built later in 2016 which will go into the main S7 fleet to replace the S7+1 set that is being retained on the Metropolitan Line. This will take the S Stock order from 191 trains to 192 trains. The two remaining S7+1 trains have an additional car each that have been 'borrowed' from two other trains. Both of the trains from which the cars were 'borrowed' were still at Bombardier in Derby as 6-car trains at the time of writing. Two additional cars are to be built during 2016 to bring these two sets back up to 7-car strength so that they can be released for traffic. Finally, when the S7+1 set which is covering for the ATC modifications reverts to 7-car formation, there will be a spare car.

Most of the sub-surface network will eventually operate automatically using a system very similar to that used on the Northern and Jubilee lines. The S Stock fleet will need to return to Bombardier in Derby to have the necessary ATC equipment fitted. This will involve the trains being hauled back to Derby over Network Rail tracks. This is also how the trains are delivered to London Underground. When trains are released from Bombardier in Derby, they are first of all taken to the Asfordby Test Centre on the Old Dalby test track in Leicestershire to undergo testing before being delivered to London, usually to Ruislip Depot. Booked haulage for these trains is four class 20s (two at each end). The class 20s couple to the S Stock via converter vehicles converted from redundant oil tank wagons. The four class 20s and the two converter vehicles give enough brake force to move the trains safely, as the S Stock's brakes are not compatible with the class 20s, and the S Stock runs unfitted (i.e.: no brakes on the S Stock itself).

20118 and 20132 lead train 7X09 through Frisby on the Wreake in Leicestershire, while working train 7X09 from the Asfordby Test Centre to Ruislip Depot on 9 December 2015. The former oil tank wagon used as a converter can be clearly seen between the rear class 20 and the S Stock set.

The train being moved was 21495-22495-24495-24496-23496-22496-21496.

Cars numbered in the 25XXX are fitted with de-icing equipment which is used to help keep the conductor rails free from ice during the winter. When this is in use, a blue light is displayed on the outside of the vehicle, as depicted here on S8 car 25010. The round blue dot after the number also denotes that the car is fitted with de-icing equipment, and this symbol is standard across all Underground trains so fitted.

55

S Stock

S Stock, 8-car (S8) Metropolitan Line

DM (D)	M1	M2	MS	MS	M2	M1	DM(A)	DM (D)	M	M	MS	MS	M	M	DM(A)
21001	22001	23001	24001	24002	25002	22002	21002	21059	22059	23059	24059	24060	23060	22060	21060
21003	22003	23003	24003	24004	25004	22004	21004	21061	22061	23061	24061	24062	23062	22062	21062
21005	22005	23005	24005	24006	25006	22006	21006	21063	22063	23063	24063	24064	23064	22064	21064
21007	22007	23007	24007	24008	25008	22008	21008	21065	22065	23065	24065	24066	23066	22066	21066
21009	22009	23009	24009	24010	25010	22010	21010	21067	22067	23067	24067	24068	23068	22068	21068
21011	22011	23011	24011	24012	25012	22012	21012	21069	22069	23069	24069	24070	23070	22070	21070
21013	22013	23013	24013	24014	25014	22014	21014	21071	22071	23071	24071	24072	23072	22072	21072
21015	22015	23015	24015	24016	25016	22016	21016	21073	22073	23073	24073	24074	23074	22074	21074
21017	22017	23017	24017	24018	25018	22018	21018	21075	22075	23075	24075	24076	23076	22076	21076
21019	22019	23019	24019	24020	25020	22020	21020	21077	22077	23077	24077	24078	23078	22078	21078
21021	22021	23021	24021	24022	25022	22022	21022	21079	22079	23079	24079	24080	23080	22080	21080
21023	22023	23023	24023	24024	25024	22024	21024	21081	22081	23081	24081	24082	23082	22082	21082
21025	22025	23025	24025	24026	25026	22026	21026	21083	22083	23083	24083	24084	23084	22084	21084
21027	22027	23027	24027	24028	25028	22028	21028	21085	22085	23085	24085	24086	23086	22086	21086
21029	22029	23029	24029	24030	25030	22030	21030	21087	22087	23087	24087	24088	23088	22088	21088
21031	22031	23031	24031	24032	25032	22032	21032	21089	22089	23089	24089	24090	23090	22090	21090
21033	22033	23033	24033	24034	25034	22034	21034	21091	22091	23091	24091	24092	23092	22092	21092
21035	22035	23035	24035	24036	25036	22036	21036	21093	22093	23093	24093	24094	23094	22094	21094
21037	22037	23037	24037	24038	25038	22038	21038	21095	22095	23095	24095	24096	23096	22096	21096
21039	22039	23039	24039	24040	25040	22040	21040	21097	22097	23097	24097	24098	23098	22098	21098
21041	22041	23041	24041	24042	25042	22042	21042	21099	22099	23099	24099	24100	23100	22100	21100
21043	22043	23043	24043	24044	25044	22044	21044	21101	22101	23101	24101	24102	23102	22102	21102
21045	22045	23045	24045	24046	25046	22046	21046	21103	22103	23103	24103	24104	23104	22104	21104
21047	22047	23047	24047	24048	25048	22048	21048	21105	22105	23105	24105	24106	23106	22106	21106
21049	22049	23049	24049	24050	25050	22050	21050	21107	22107	23107	24107	24108	23108	22108	21108
21051	22051	23051	24051	24052	25052	22052	21052	21109	22109	23109	24109	24110	23110	22110	21110
21053	22053	23053	24053	24054	25054	22054	21054	21111	22111	23111	24111	24112	23112	22112	21112
21055	22055	23055	24055	24056	25056	22056	21056	21113	22113	23113	24113	24114	23114	22114	21114
21057	22057	23057	24057	24058	23058	22058	21058	21115	22115	23115	24115	24116	23116	22116	21116

S Stock, 7-car (S7) Circle, District and Hammersmith & City lines, and 8-car (S7+1) Metropolitan line (highlighted in yellow)

DM(D)	M1	M2	MS	MS	M	M	DM(A)	DM(D)	M1	MS	MS	M2	M1	DM(A)
21301	22301		24301	24302	25302	22302	21302	21331	22331	24331	24332	25332	22332	21332
21303	22303		24303	24304	25304	22304	21304	21333	22333	24333	24334	25334	22334	21334
21305	22305		24305	24306	25306	22306	21306	21335	22335	24335	24336	25336	22336	21336
21307	22307		24307	24308	25308	22308	21308	21337	22337	24337	24338	25338	22338	21338
21309	22309		24309	24310	25310	22310	21310	21339	22339	24339	24340	25340	22340	21340
21311	22311		24311	24312	25312	22312	21312	21341	22341	24341	24342	25342	22342	21342
21313	22313		24313	24314	25314	22314	21314	21343	22343	24343	24344	25344	22344	21344
21315	22315		24315	24316	25316	22316	21316	21345	22345	24345	24346	25346	22346	21346
21317	22317		24317	24318	25318	22318	21318	21347	22347	24347	24348	25348	22348	21348
21319	22319		24319	24320	25320	22320	21320	21349	22349	24349	24350	25350	22350	21350
21311	22311		24311	24312	25312	22312	21312	21351	22351	24351	24352	25352	22352	21352
21313	22313		24313	24314	25314	22314	21314	21353	22353	24353	24354	25354	22354	21354
21315	22315		24315	24316	25316	22316	21316	21355	22355	24355	24356	25356	22356	21356
21317	22317		24317	24318	25318	22318	21318	21357	22357	24357	24358	25358	22358	21358
21319	22319	25382	24319	24320	25320	22320	21320	21359	22359	24359	24360	25360	22360	21360
21321	22321		24321	24322	25322	22322	21322	21361	22361	24361	24362	25362	22362	21362
21323	22323	25384	24323	24324	25324	22324	21324	21363	22363	24363	24364	25364	22364	21364
21325	22325		24325	24326	25326	22326	21326	21365	22365	24365	24366	25366	22366	21366
21327	22327	25386	24327	24328	25328	22328	21328	21367	22367	24367	24368	25368	22368	21368
21329	22329		24329	24330	25330	22330	21330	21369	22369	24369	24370	25370	22370	21370

S Stock

S Stock, 7-car (S7) Circle, District and Hammersmith & City lines

DM(D)	M	MS	MS	M	M	DM(A)	DM(D)	M	MS	MS	M	M	DM(A)
21371	22371	24371	24372	25372	22372	21372	21469	22469	24469	24470	23470	22470	21470
21373	22373	24373	24374	25374	22374	21374	21471	22471	24471	24472	23472	22472	21472
21375	22375	24375	24376	25376	22376	21376	21473	22473	24473	24474	23474	22474	21474
21377	22377	24377	24378	25378	22378	21378	21475	22475	24475	24476	23476	22476	21476
21379	22379	24379	24380	25380	22380	21380	21477	22477	24477	24478	23478	22478	21478
21381	*22381*	*24381*	*24382*	*(25382)*	*22382*	*21382*	21479	22479	24479	24480	23480	22480	21480
21383	*22383*	*24383*	*24384*	*XXXXX*	*22384*	*21384*	21481	22481	24481	24482	23482	22482	21482
21385	*22385*	*24385*	*24386*	*XXXXX*	*22386*	*21386*	21483	22483	24483	24484	23484	22484	21484
21387	22387	24387	24388	23388	22388	21388	21485	22485	24485	24486	23486	22486	21486
21389	22389	24389	24390	23390	22390	21390	21487	22487	24487	24488	23488	22488	21488
21391	22391	24391	24392	23392	22392	21392	21489	22489	24489	24490	23490	22490	21490
21393	22393	24393	24394	23394	22394	21394	21491	22491	24491	24492	23492	22492	21492
21395	22395	24395	24396	23396	22396	21396	21493	22493	24493	24494	23494	22494	21494
21397	22397	24397	24398	23398	22398	21398	21495	22495	24495	24496	23496	22496	21496
21399	22399	24399	24400	23400	22400	21400	21497	22497	24497	24498	23498	22498	21498
21401	22401	24401	24402	23402	22402	21402	21499	22499	24499	24500	23500	22500	21500
21403	22403	24403	24404	23404	22404	21404	*21501*	*22501*	*24501*	*24502*	*23502*	*22502*	*21502*
21405	22405	24405	24406	23406	22406	21406	21503	22503	24503	24504	23504	22504	21504
21407	22407	24407	24408	23408	22408	21408	21505	22505	24505	24506	23506	22506	21506
21409	22409	24409	24410	23410	22410	21410	21507	22507	24507	24508	23508	22508	21508
21411	22411	24411	24412	23412	22412	21412	21509	22509	24509	24510	23510	22510	21510
21413	22413	24413	24414	23414	22414	21414	21511	22511	24511	24512	23512	22512	21512
21415	22415	24415	24416	23416	22416	21416	*21513*	*22513*	*24513*	*24514*	*23514*	*22514*	*21514*
21417	22417	24417	24418	23418	22418	21418	*21515*	*22515*	*24515*	*24516*	*23516*	*22516*	*21516*
21419	22419	24419	24420	23420	22420	21420	*21517*	*22517*	*24517*	*24518*	*23518*	*22518*	*21518*
21421	22421	24421	24422	23422	22422	21422	*21519*	*22519*	*24519*	*24520*	*23520*	*22520*	*21520*
21423	22423	24423	24424	23424	22424	21424	*21521*	*22521*	*24521*	*24522*	*23522*	*22522*	*21522*
21425	22425	24425	24426	23426	22426	21426	*21523*	*22523*	*24523*	*24524*	*23524*	*22524*	*21524*
21427	22427	24427	24428	23428	22428	21428	*21525*	*22525*	*24525*	*24526*	*23526*	*22526*	*21526*
21429	22429	24429	24430	23430	22430	21430	*21527*	*22527*	*24527*	*24528*	*23528*	*22528*	*21528*
21431	22431	24431	24432	23432	22432	21432	*21529*	*22529*	*24529*	*24530*	*23530*	*22530*	*21530*
21433	22433	24433	24434	23434	22434	21434	*21531*	*22531*	*24531*	*24532*	*23532*	*22532*	*21532*
21435	22435	24435	24436	23436	22436	21436	*21533*	*22533*	*24533*	*24534*	*23534*	*22534*	*21534*
21437	22437	24437	24438	23438	22438	21438	*21535*	*22535*	*24535*	*24536*	*23536*	*22536*	*21536*
21439	22439	24439	24440	23440	22440	21440	*21537*	*22537*	*24537*	*24538*	*23538*	*22538*	*21538*
21441	22441	24441	24442	23442	22442	21442	*21539*	*22539*	*24539*	*24540*	*23540*	*22540*	*21540*
21443	22443	24443	24444	23444	22444	21444	*21541*	*22541*	*24541*	*24542*	*23542*	*22542*	*21542*
21445	22445	24445	24446	23446	22446	21446	*21543*	*22543*	*24543*	*24544*	*23544*	*22544*	*21544*
21447	22447	24447	24448	23448	22448	21448	*21545*	*22545*	*24545*	*24546*	*23546*	*22546*	*21546*
21449	22449	24449	24450	23450	22450	21450	*21547*	*22547*	*24547*	*24548*	*23548*	*22548*	*21548*
21451	22451	24451	24452	23452	22452	21452	*21549*	*22549*	*24549*	*24550*	*23550*	*22550*	*21550*
21453	22453	24453	24454	23454	22454	21454	*21551*	*22551*	*24551*	*24552*	*23552*	*22552*	*21552*
21455	22455	24455	24456	23456	22456	21456	*21553*	*22553*	*24553*	*24554*	*23554*	*22554*	*21554*
21457	22457	24457	24458	23458	22458	21458	*21555*	*22555*	*24555*	*24556*	*23556*	*22556*	*21556*
21459	22459	24459	24460	23460	22460	21460	*21557*	*22557*	*24557*	*24558*	*23558*	*22558*	*21558*
21461	22461	24461	24462	23462	22462	21462	*21559*	*22559*	*24559*	*24560*	*23560*	*22560*	*21560*
21463	22463	24463	24464	23464	22464	21464	*21561*	*22561*	*24561*	*24562*	*23562*	*22562*	*21562*
21465	22465	24465	24466	23466	22466	21466	*21563*	*22563*	*24563*	*24564*	*23564*	*22564*	*21564*
21467	*22467*	*24467*	*24468*	*23468*	*22468*	*21468*	*21565*	*22565*	*24565*	*24566*	*23566*	*22566*	*21566*
							21567*	*22567**	*24567**	*24568**	*23568**	*22568**	*21568**

Bold and italics - not on LU

The two cars highlighted in yellow and marked 'XXXXX' are the cars that have been transferred into units 21323-21324 and 21327-21328 to make them up to 8 cars. These cars will be replaced, but the numbers to be carried by these cars are not yet known.

The final train marked '*' is the additional (192nd) train, the numbering of which was still to be confirmed at the time of writing, although it is expected to follow on from the rest of the fleet.

1972 Stock

1972 STOCK

Size of stock: Tube
Year of manufacture: 1972-1974
Built by: Metro-Cammell, Birmingham
Entry into service: 1972
Lines used on: Bakerloo
Number of cars per train: 7
Train formation: DM-T-T-DM+UNDM-T-DM plus one train formed DM-T-T-UNDM+UNDM-T-DM

Led by unit 3260-4260-4360-3360, a southbound train arrives at Kilburn Park on 25 November 2015.

First introduced to the Northern Line in 1972, the first batch of 1972 Stock later became known as 1972 MkI Stock. A later batch, intended for eventual use on the Jubilee Line, was introduced in 1973, and these became known as 1972 MkII Stock. They were built as a crew operated (i.e.: driver and guard) version of the automatic, and almost identical externally, 1967 Stock on the Victoria Line (now withdrawn). After use on the Northern and Jubilee lines, all of the 1972 MkII Stock was moved to the Bakerloo Line. Mixed in amongst the MkII cars are a number of MkI cars that have been incorporated into the MkII fleet and renumbered. Although they are pretty much identical, look out for black handles on the ventilation grilles and internal panels with a black pattern instead of brown inside some of the ex MkI cars. Don't be too surprised to see the occasional blue ventilation grille handle or grab rail, no doubt spare parts obtained from the withdrawn Victoria Line 1967 fleet.

The trains are formed of two units back to back, a 4-car unit at the south end, and a 3-car unit at the north end. All of the four-car units have a DM at both ends, except one unit which has a UNDM instead. This unit is numbered out of sequence (3299-4299-4399-3399) to highlight to operational staff that it is different.

Since the withdrawal of the C Stock, the 1972 Stock is now the oldest type of train in regular passenger use. It is planned eventually to replace the 1972 Stock with the 'New Tube for London', but this is likely to be many years away (2033 has been suggested), so the 1972 Stock will need to soldier

1972 Stock

on for a few more years yet. In order to achieve this expected extended life, the fleet is currently undergoing life extension work at Acton Works. This mostly involves repairs to rotten areas of the bodywork and under-frames, but a new moquette seat covering is likely to start appearing during 2016.

The interior of UNDM 3438 clearly showing a brown Bakerloo grab rail and a Victoria Line blue grab rail. Photo taken on 25 November 2015.

1972 MkII Stock (Bakerloo line)
4-car 'A' end units (south facing)

DM(A)	T	T	DM(D)	DM(A)	T	T	DM(D)	DM(A)	T	T	DM(D)	DM(A)	T	T	DM(D)
3231	4231	4331	3331	3240	4240	4340	3340	3250	4250	4350	3350	3260	4260	4360	3360
3232	4232	4332	3332	3241	4241	4341	3341	3251	4251	4351	3351	3261	4261	4361	3361
3233	4233	4333	3333	3242	4242	4342	3342	3252	4252	4352	3352	3262	4262	4362	3362
3234	4234	4334	3334	3243	4243	4343	3343	3253	4253	4353	3353	3263	4263	4363	3363
3235	4235	4335	3335	3244	4244	4344	3344	3254	4254	4354	3354	3264*	4264*	4364*	3364*
3236	4236	4336	3336	3245	4245	4345	3345	3255	4255	4355	3355	3265*	4265*	4365*	3365*
3237	4237	4337	3337	3246	4246	4346	3346	3256	4256	4356	3356	3266*	4266*	4366	3366
3238	4238	4338	3338	3247	4247	4347	3347	3258	4258	4358	3358	3267*	4267*	4367*	3367*
3239	4239	4339	3339	3248	4248	4348	3348	3259	4259	4359	3359				

DM(A)	T	T	UNDM
3299	4299	4399	3399

3-car 'D' end units (north facing)

UNDM	T	DM(D)	UNDM	T	DM(D)	UNDM	T	DM(D)	UNDM	T	DM(D)	UNDM	T	DM(D)
3431	4531	3531	3438	4538	3538	3446	4546	3546	3453	4553	3553	3460	4560	3560
3432	4532	3532	3440	4540	3540	3447	4547	3547	3454	4554	3554	3461	4561	3561
3433	4533	3533	3441	4541	3541	3448	4548	3548	3455	4555	3555	3462	4562	3562
3434	4534	3534	3442	4542	3542	3449	4549	3549	3456	4556	3556	3463	4563	3563
3435	4535	3535	3443	4543	3543	3450	4550	3550	3457	4557	3557	3464*	4564*	3564*
3436	4536	3536	3444	4544	3544	3451	4551	3551	3458	4558	3558	3465*	4565*	3565*
3437	4537	3537	3445	4545	3545	3452	4552	3552	3459	4559	3559	3466*	4566*	3566*
												3467*	4567*	3567*

* 1972 MkI stock cars renumbered

1973 Stock

1973 STOCK

Size of stock: Tube
Year of manufacture: 1974-1977
Built by: Metro-Cammell, Birmingham
Entry into service: 1975
Lines used on: Piccadilly
Number of cars per train: 6
Train formation: DM-T-UNDM+UNDM-T-DM or DM-T-DM+UNDM-T-DM
or DM-T-UNDM+DM-T-DM or DM-T-DM+DM-T-DM

The 1973 Stock was built to coincide with the extending of the Piccadilly Line to Heathrow Airport, with the first trains entering service in 1975. The interiors were designed with Heathrow passenger traffic in mind, and there is space adjacent to the doors where large luggage can be accommodated. Each train is made up of two three car units. Most of these are singled ended with a UNDM on the inner end, but there are also 21 double ended units to give greater operational flexibility. Trains can be made up of two single ended units, two double ended units or a single ended unit and a double ended unit. The single ended units are designated as 'A' end or 'D' end units, but due to the Heathrow Terminal 4 loop, trains are repeatedly turned and trains do not always face in the same direction. The 1973 Stock fleet was refurbished between 1995 and 2000 and is expected to last into the 2020s when it is expected that replacement will come in the form of the 'New Tube for London'.

Above: Unit 224-624-424 arrives into Hammersmith with a Cockfosters bound service as a westbound train departs, 19 December 2015.

Opposite: At the time of compiling this book, one train of 1973 Stock was in service carrying a vinyl wrap advertising the 'Night Tube'. In this view, the train is seen arriving at Manor House with a service for Northfields on 25 July 2015. The unit is formed 103-503-303+452-652-252.

1973 Stock

1973 Stock (Piccadilly line)
3-car 'A' end units

DM(A)	T	UNDM	DM(A)	T	UNDM	DM(A)	T	UNDM	DM(A)	T	UNDM	DM(A)	T	UNDM
100	500	300	128	528	328	154	554	354	182	582	382	210	610	410	236	636	436
102	502	302	130	530	330	156	556	356	184	584	384	212	612	412	238	638	438
104	504	304	132	532	332	158	558	358	186	586	386	214	614	414	240	640	440
106	506	306	134	534	334	160	560	360	188	588	388	216	616	416	242	642	442
108	508	308	136	536	336	162	562	362	190	590	390	218	618	418	244	644	444
110	510	310	138	538	338	164	564	364	192	592	392	220	620	420	246	646	446
112	512	312	140	540	340	168	568	368	194	594	394	222	622	422	248	648	448
116	516	316	142	542	342	170	570	370	196	596	396	224	624	424	250	650	450
118	518	318	144	544	344	172	572	372	198	598	398	226	626	426	252	652	452
120	520	320	146	546	346	174	574	374	200	600	400	228	628	428			
122	522	322	148	548	348	176	576	376	202	602	402	230	630	430			
124	524	324	150	550	350	178	578	378	206	606	406	232	632	432			
126	526	326	152	552	352	180	580	380	208	608	408	234	634	434			

1973 Stock (Piccadilly line)
3-car 'D' end units

UNDM	T	DM(D)	UNDM	T	DM(D)	UNDM	T	DM(D)	UNDM	T	DM(D)	UNDM	T	DM(D)	UNDM	T	DM(D)
301	501	101	327	527	127	353	553	153	379	579	179	405	605	205	431	631	231
303	503	103	329	529	129	355	555	155	381	581	181	407	607	207	433	633	233
305	505	105	331	531	131	357	557	157	383	583	183	409	609	209	435	635	235
307	507	107	333	533	133	359	559	159	385	585	185	411	611	211	437	637	237
309	509	109	335	535	135	361	561	161	387	587	187	413	613	213	439	639	239
311	511	111	337	537	137	363	563	163	389	589	189	415	615	215	441	641	241
313	513	113	339	539	139	365	565	165	391	591	191	417	617	217	443	643	243
315	515	115	341	541	141	367	567	167	393	593	193	419	619	219	445	645	245
317	517	117	343	543	143	369	569	169	395	595	195	421	621	221	447	647	247
319	519	119	345	545	145	371	571	171	397	597	197	423	623	223	449	649	249
321	521	121	347	547	147	373	573	173	399	599	199	425	625	225	451	651	251
323	523	123	349	549	149	375	575	175	401	601	201	427	627	227	453	653	253
325	525	125	351	551	151	377	577	177	403	603	203	429	629	229			

1973 Stock (Piccadilly line)
3-car double ended units

DM(A)	T	DM(D)	DM(A)	T	DM(D)	DM(A)	T	DM(D)	DM(A)	T	DM(D)	DM(A)	T	DM(D)	DM(A)	T	DM(D)
854	654	855	862	662	863	870	670	871	878	678	879	886	686	887	896	696	897
856	656	857	864	664	865	872	672	873	880	680	881	890	690	891			
858	658	859	866	666	867	874	674	875	882	682	883	892	692	893			
860	660	861	868	668	869	876	676	877	884	684	885	894	694	895			

61

1992 Stock

1992 STOCK

Size of stock: Tube
Year of manufacture: 1991-1994
Built by: BREL (Adtranz), Derby
Entry into service: 1993 (on both the Central and Waterloo & City)
Lines used on: Central and Waterloo & City
Number of cars per train: 8 (Central) / 4 (Waterloo & City)
Train formation: see explanation below

A westbound Central Line service arrives at Marble Arch led by 91283 on 18 October 2015.

The 1992 Stock was the result of extensive testing of three prototype trains of 1986 Stock. They were introduced onto the Central Line from 1993 to replace the driver and guard operated 1962 Stock. British Rail (Network Southeast) tagged five 4-car sets onto the order to replace the class 487 units then in use on the Waterloo & City Line (which at the time was not a part of the London Underground). The Waterloo & City Line units were designated class 482 and were finished in a version of the Network Southeast red, white and blue livery. In 1994, the Waterloo & City became a part of London Underground, and the class 482s were painted in the standard London Underground red, white and blue livery in 2006, and are now known as 1992 Stock. The Waterloo & City is of course totally isolated from the rest of the London Underground network, so there is no scope for the two fleets ever to operate together. On the Central Line, the 1992 Stock runs as 8-car trains made up of four 2-car units. The Central Line fleet is designed to be totally reversible and 2-car units can be formed as A+B, B+C or B+D (A = DM / B and C = NDM / D = de-icing NDM). These 2-car units can be formed into any of 36 different combinations to make up an 8-car train, so long as the A cars are at the outer ends. On the Waterloo & City Line, trains are formed DM-NDM+NDM-DM.

The Central Line is an automatic railway and the 1992 Stock operates with the Automatic Train Operation (ATO) driving the trains and the Automatic Train Protection (ATP) picking up codes in the track to determine target speeds. They can also operate in coded manual, where the train operator drives the train manually but obeys the target speeds set by the ATP. There is also a restricted manual

1992 Stock

mode where the train is driven manually with the ATP isolated and the train operator obeys trackside signals. In this mode, the train is restricted to 11mph. The Waterloo & City Line trains are driven manually as the Waterloo & City is fitted with colour light signals and train stops. As there are only two stations on the Waterloo & City, the trains have fixed destinations displayed on the cab fronts, Bank on one end and Waterloo on the other end.

During 2011 and 2012, the Central Line fleet underwent a refresh and received new saloon windows, a new seat moquette, new internal lighting and modified cab fronts.

Interior view of a Central Line 'B' car (NDM).

1992 Stock (Central Line)
2-car A-B units

DM(A)	NDM(B)	DM(A)	NDM(B)	DM(A)	NDM(B)	DM(A)	NDM(B)	DM(A)	NDM(B)	DM(A)	NDM(B)
91001	92001	91057	92057	91113	92113	91169	92169	91225	92225	91281	92281	91337	92337
91003	92003	91059	92059	91115	92115	91171	92171	91227	92227	91283	92283	91339	92339
91005	92005	91061	92061	91117	92117	91173	92173	91229	92229	91285	92285	91341	92341
91007	92007	91063	92063	91119	92119	91175	92175	91231	92231	91287	92287	91343	92343
91009	92009	91065	92065	91121	92121	91177	92177	91233	92233	91289	92289	91345	92345
91011	92011	91067	92067	91123	92123	91179	92179	91235	92235	91291	92291	91347	92347
91013	92013	91069	92069	91125	92125	91181	92181	91237	92237	91293	92293	91349	92349
91015	92015	91071	92071	91127	92127	91183	92183	91239	92239	91295	92295		
91017	92017	91073	92073	91129	92129	91185	92185	91241	92241	91297	92297		
91019	92019	91075	92075	91131	92131	91187	92187	91243	92243	91299	92299		
91021	92021	91077	92077	91133	92133	91189	92189	91245	92245	91301	92301		
91023	92023	91079	92079	91135	92135	91191	92191	91247	92247	91303	92303		
91025	92025	91081	92081	91137	92137	91193	92193	91249	92249	91305	92305		
91027	92027	91083	92083	91139	92139	91195	92195	91251	92251	91307	92307		
91029	92029	91085	92085	91141	92141	91197	92197	91253	92253	91309	92309		
91031	92031	91087	92087	91143	92143	91199	92199	91255	92255	91311	92311		
91033	92033	91089	92089	91145	92145	91201	92201	91257	92257	91313	92313		
91035	92035	91091	92091	91147	92147	91203	92203	91259	92259	91315	92315		
91037	92037	91093	92093	91149	92149	91205	92205	91261	92261	91317	92317		
91039	92039	91095	92095	91151	92151	91207	92207	91263	92263	91319	92319		
91041	92041	91097	92097	91153	92153	91209	92209	91265	92265	91321	92321		
91043	92043	91099	92099	91155	92155	91211	92211	91267	92267	91323	92323		
91045	92045	91101	92101	91157	92157	91213	92213	91269	92269	91325	92325		
91047	92047	91103	92103	91159	92159	91215	92215	91271	92271	91327	92327		
91049	92049	91105	92105	91161	92161	91217	92217	91273	92273	91329	92329		
91051	92051	91107	92107	91163	92163	91219	92219	91275	92275	91331	92331		
91053	92053	91109	92109	91165	92165	91221	92221	91277	92277	91333	92333		
91055	92055	91111	92111	91167	92167	91223	92223	91279	92279	91335	92335		

1992 Stock (Waterloo & City line)

2-car units (facing Bank)		2-car units (facing Waterloo)	
DM	NDM	NDM	DM
65501	67501	67502	65502
65503	67503	67504	65504
65505	67505	67506	65506
65507	67507	67508	65508
65509	67509	67510	65510

63

1992 Stock

1992 Stock (Central Line)
2-car A-B units

NDM(B)	NDM (C)	NDM(B)	NDM (C)	NDM(B)	NDM (C)	NDM(B)	NDM (C)	NDM(B)	NDM (C)
92002	93002	92042	93042	92082	93082	92122	93122	92162	93162
92004	93004	92044	93044	92084	93084	92124	93124	92164	93164
92006	93006	92046	93046	92086	93086	92126	93126	92166	93166
92008	93008	92048	93048	92088	93088	92128	93128	92168	93168
92010	93010	92050	93050	92090	93090	92130	93130	92170	93170
92012	93012	92052	93052	92092	93092	92132	93132	92172	93172
92014	93014	92054	93054	92094	93094	92134	93134	92174	93174
92016	93016	92056	93056	92096	93096	92136	93136	92176	93176
92018	93018	92058	93058	92098	93098	92138	93138	92178	93178
92020	93020	92060	93060	92100	93100	92140	93140	92180	93180
92022	93022	92062	93062	92102	93102	92142	93142	92182	93182
92024	93024	92064	93064	92104	93104	92144	93144	92184	93184
92026	93026	92066	93066	92106	93106	92146	93146	92186	93186
92028	93028	92068	93068	92108	93108	92148	93148	92188	93188
92030	93030	92070	93070	92110	93110	92150	93150	92190	93190
92032	93032	92072	93072	92112	93112	92152	93152	92192	93192
92034	93034	92074	93074	92114	93114	92154	93154	92194	93194
92036	93036	92076	93076	92116	93116	92156	93156	92196	93196
92038	93038	92078	93078	92118	93118	92158	93158	92198	93198
92040	93040	92080	93080	92120	93120	92160	93160	92200	93200

NDM(B)	NDM (C)	NDM(B)	NDM (C)
92202	93202	92242	93242
92204	93204	92244	93244
92206	93206	92246	93246
92208	93208	92248	93248
92210	93210	92250	93250
92212	93212	92252	93252
92214	93214	92254	93254
92216	93216	92256	93256
92218	93218	92258	93258
92220	93220	92260	93260
92222	93222	92262	93262
92224	93224	92264	93264
92226	93226	92266	93266
92228	93228		
92230	93230		
92232	93232		
92234	93234		
92236	93236		
92238	93238		
92240	93240		

1992 Stock (Central Line)
2-car B-D de-icing units

NDM(B)	NDM (D)	NDM(B)	NDM (D)	NDM(B)	NDM (D)	NDM(B)	NDM (D)	NDM(B)	NDM (D)	NDM(B)	NDM (D)
92402	93402	92412	93412	92422	93422	92432	93432	92442	93442	92452	93452
92404	93404	92414	93414	92424	93424	92434	93434	92444	93444	92454	93454
92406	93406	92416	93416	92426	93426	92436	93436	92446	93446	92456	93456
92408	93408	92418	93418	92428	93428	92438	93438	92448	93448	92458	93458
92410	93410	92420	93420	92430	93430	92440	93440	92450	93450	92460	93460

NDM(B)	NDM (D)
92462	93462
92464	93464

For a short period during 2015, Waterloo & City Line train 65503-67503+67504-65504 carried an all over vinyl wrap advert for the Rugby World Cup. The seat moquette throughout the train was also changed for a moquette advertising one of the main sponsors of the event. The vinyl wrap and seat moquette was removed at the beginning of November 2015. In this view, the train is leaving the set down only platform at Waterloo and is heading into Waterloo depot to reverse. 31 October 2015.

1995 Stock

1995 STOCK

Size of stock: Tube
Year of manufacture: 1996-1999
Built by: Alsthom Transportation, Birmingham
Entry into service: 1998
Lines used on: Northern
Number of cars per train: 6
Train formation: DM-T-UNDM+UNDM-T-DM

A High Barnet to Kennington (via Charing Cross) service arrives at Finchley Central with 'A' end unit 51518-52518-53518 leading on 16 May 2015.

The 1995 Stock was introduced to the Northern Line from 1998 onwards to replace the older crew operated (driver and guard) trains of 1959 Stock and 1972 Stock. In January 2000, the old stock had been eradicated. When first introduced, the 1995 Stock operated in one person only (OPO) mode, but they were manually driven as the Northern Line was signalled throughout with colour light signals fitted with train stops. The signalling has since been upgraded and since 2014, has been operated automatically using the Transmission Based Train Control System (TBTC).

Although designated as 1995 Stock, they were in fact built from 1996 onwards alongside the Jubilee Line's 1996 Stock. They look almost identical to their Jubilee Line relatives, and were classified as 1995 Stock to distinguish them from the 1996 Stock. Beneath the skin, the 1995 Stock is very different from the 1996 Stock and has a more modern traction package than the 1996 Stock. The 1995 Stock has Alsthom's 'Onyx' three phase Insulated Gate Bipolar Transistor system (IGBT) which makes a very different sound to the traction package on the 1996 Stock which employs Gate Turn Off Thyristors (GTOs).

The trains also differ internally, with the 1996 Stock having perch seats alongside the doors, while the 1995 Stock has tip up seats. 2015 saw the completion of a refresh for the 1995 Stock which saw their cabs and interiors refurbished and LED destination displays fitted.

1995 Stock

Interior view of a 1995 Stock driving motor, clearly showing the tip up seats adjacent to the doors.

1995 Stock (Northern line)
3-car 'A' end units

DM(A)	T	UNDM	DM(A)	T	UNDM	DM(A)	T	UNDM	DM(A)	T	UNDM	DM(A)	T	UNDM
51502	52502	53502	51540	52540	53540	51578	52578	53578	51616	52616	53616	51654	52654	53654
51504	52504	53504	51542	52542	53542	51580	52580	53580	51618	52618	53618	51656	52656	53656
51506	52506	53506	51544	52544	53544	51582	52582	53582	51620	52620	53620	51658	52658	53658
51508	52508	53508	51546	52546	53546	51584	52584	53584	51622	52622	53622	51660	52660	53660
51510	52510	53510	51548	52548	53548	51586	52586	53586	51624	52624	53624	51662	52662	53662
51512	52512	53512	51550	52550	53550	51588	52588	53588	51626	52626	53626	51664	52664	53664
51514	52514	53514	51552	52552	53552	51590	52590	53590	51628	52628	53628	51666	52666	53666
51516	52516	53516	51554	52554	53554	51592	52592	53592	51630	52630	53630	51668	52668	53668
51518	52518	53518	51556	52556	53556	51594	52594	53594	51632	52632	53632	51670	52670	53670
51520	52520	53520	51558	52558	53558	51596	52596	53596	51634	52634	53634	51672	52672	53672
51522	52522	53522	51560	52560	53560	51598	52598	53598	51636	52636	53636	51674	52674	53674
51524	52524	53524	51562	52562	53562	51600	52600	53600	51638	52638	53638	51676	52676	53676
51526	52526	53526	51564	52564	53564	51602	52602	53602	51640	52640	53640	51678	52678	53678
51528	52528	53528	51566	52566	53566	51604	52604	53604	51642	52642	53642	51680	52680	53680
51530	52530	53530	51568	52568	53568	51606	52606	53606	51644	52644	53644	51682	52682	53682
51532	52532	53532	51570	52570	53570	51608	52608	53608	51646	52646	53646	51684	52684	53684
51534	52534	53534	51572	52572	53572	51610	52610	53610	51648	52648	53648	51686	52686	53686
51536	52536	53536	51574	52574	53574	51612	52612	53612	51650	52650	53650			
51538	52538	53538	51576	52576	53576	51614	52614	53614	51652	52652	53652			

1995 Stock (Northern line)
3-car 'D' end units

UNDM	T	DM(D)	UNDM	T	DM(D)	UNDM	T	DM(D)	UNDM	T	DM(D)	UNDM	T	DM(D)
53501	52501	51501	53539	52539	51539	53577	52577	51577	53615	52615	51615	53653	52653	51653
53503	52503	51503	53541	52541	51541	53579	52579	51579	53617	52617	51617	53655	52655	51655
53505	52505	51505	53543	52543	51543	53581	52581	51581	53619	52619	51619	53657	52657	51657
53507	52507	51507	53545	52545	51545	53583	52583	51583	53621	52621	51621	53659	52659	51659
53509	52509	51509	53547	52547	51547	53585	52585	51585	53623	52623	51623	53661	52661	51661
53511	52511	51511	53549	52549	51549	53587	52587	51587	53625	52625	51625	53663	52663	51663
53513	52513	51513	53551	52551	51551	53589	52589	51589	53627	52627	51627	53665	52665	51665
53515	52515	51515	53553	52553	51553	53591	52591	51591	53629	52629	51629	53667	52667	51667
53517	52517	51517	53555	52555	51555	53593	52593	51593	53631	52631	51631	53669	52669	51669
53519	52519	51519	53557	52557	51557	53595	52595	51595	53633	52633	51633	53671	52671	51671
53521	52521	51521	53559	52559	51559	53597	52597	51597	53635	52635	51635	53673	52673	51673
53523	52523	51523	53561	52561	51561	53599	52599	51599	53637	52637	51637	53675	52675	51675
53525	52525	51525	53563	52563	51563	53601	52601	51601	53639	52639	51639	53677	52677	51677
53527	52527	51527	53565	52565	51565	53603	52603	51603	53641	52641	51641	53679	52679	51679
53529	52529	51529	53567	52567	51567	53605	52605	51605	53643	52643	51643	53681	52681	51681
53531	52531	51531	53569	52569	51569	53607	52607	51607	53645	52645	51645	53683	52683	51683
53533	52533	51533	53571	52571	51571	53609	52609	51609	53647	52647	51647	53685	52685	51685
53535	52535	51535	53573	52573	51573	53611	52611	51611	53649	52649	51649			
53537	52537	51537	53575	52575	51575	53613	52613	51613	53651	52651	51651			

1996 Stock

1995 Stock (Northern line)											
3-car 'A' end de-icing units											
DM(A)	T	UNDM	DM(A)	T	UNDM	DM(A)	T	UNDM	DM(A)	T	UNDM
51702	52702	53702	51708	52708	53708	51714	52714	53714	51720	52720	53720	51726	52726	53726
51704	52704	53704	51710	52710	53710	51716	52716	53716	51722	52722	53722
51706	52706	53706	51712	52712	53712	51718	52718	53718	51724	52724	53724

1995 Stock (Northern line)											
3-car 'D' end de-icing units											
UNDM	T	DM(D)	UNDM	T	DM(D)	UNDM	T	DM(D)	UNDM	T	DM(D)	UNDM	T	DM(D)
53701	52701	51701	53707	52707	51707	53713	52713	51713	53719	52719	51719	53725	52725	51725
53703	52703	51703	53709	52709	51709	53715	52715	51715	53721	52721	51721
53705	52705	51705	53711	52711	51711	53717	52717	51717	53723	52723	51723

1996 STOCK

Size of stock: Tube
Year of manufacture: 1996-1999 and 2005-2006
Built by: Alsthom Transportation, Birmingham
Entry into service: 1997
Lines used on: Jubilee
Number of cars per train: 7
Train formation: DM-T-UNDM+UNDM-T-T-DM

The 1996 Stock was built to serve the Jubilee Line Extension (JLE). When introduced, the Jubilee Line was being served by trains of relatively new 1983 Stock, which were not deemed to be suitable for operation over the new line. The introduction of the 1996 Stock saw the withdrawal of the 1983 Stock, which never found any further use elsewhere on the Underground. The 1996 Stock entered

A Stanmore bound Jubilee Line service arrives at Bond Street with 96014 leading on 27 December 2015.

1996 Stock

service between December 1997 and July 2001 as 6-car trains. In 2005/6 new trailer cars were delivered to bring the fleet up to 7-cars, together with four additional trains that were delivered as 7-car trains.

While very similar externally to the Northern Line's 1995 Stock, the 1996 Stock has a very different traction package using Gate Turn Off Thyristors (GTOs) similar to the equipment used on class 465 Networker EMUs. This gives the 1996 Stock a very distinctive sound which changes tone as the train accelerates or decelerates, whereas the 1995 Stock has a slightly quieter and more constant tone.

When first introduced, the Jubilee Line was still fitted with colour light signals protected by train stops and trains were driven manually. The line has since been resignalled using the Transmission Based Train Control 'moving block' system (TBTC), which was implemented in two stages, Dollis Hill to Stratford and Charing Cross (29 December 2010), and Dollis Hill to Stanmore (26 June 2011).

1996 Stock (Jubilee line)
3-car 'A' end units

DM(A)	T	UNDM	DM(A)	T	UNDM	DM(A)	T	UNDM	DM(A)	T	UNDM	DM(A)	T	UNDM
96002	96202	96402	96028	96228	96428	96054	96254	96454	96080	96880	96480	96106	96906	96506
96004	96204	96404	96030	96230	96430	96056	96256	96456	96082	96882	96482	96108	96908	96508
96006	96206	96406	96032	96232	96432	96058	96258	96458	96084	96884	96484	96110	96910	96510
96008	96208	96408	96034	96234	96434	96060	96260	96460	96086	96886	96486	96112	96912	96512
96010	96210	96410	96036	96236	96436	96062	96262	96462	96088	96888	96488	96114	96914	96514
96012	96212	96412	96038	96238	96438	96064	96264	96464	96090	96890	96490	96116	96916	96516
96014	96214	96414	96040	96240	96440	96066	96266	96466	96092	96892	96492	96118	96918	96518
96016	96216	96416	96042	96242	96442	96068	96268	96468	96094	96894	96494	96120	96320	96520
96018	96218	96418	96044	96244	96444	96070	96270	96470	96096	96896	96496	96122	96322	96522
96020	96220	96420	96046	96246	96446	96072	96272	96472	96098	96898	96498	96124	96324	96524
96022	96222	96422	96048	96248	96448	96074	96274	96474	96100	96900	96500	96126	96326	96526
96024	96224	96424	96050	96250	96450	96076	96276	96476	96102	96902	96502			
96026	96226	96426	96052	96252	96452	96078	96278	96478	96104	96904	96504			

1996 Stock (Jubilee line)
4-car 'D' end units

UNDM	T	T	DM(D)	UNDM	T	T	DM(D)	UNDM	T	T	DM(D)	UNDM	T	T	DM(D)
96401	96601	96201	96001	96433	96633	96233	96033	96465	96665	96265	96065	96497	96697	96297	96097
96403	96603	96203	96003	96435	96635	96235	96035	96467	96667	96267	96067	96499	96699	96299	96099
96405	96605	96205	96005	96437	96637	96237	96037	96469	96669	96269	96069	96501	96701	96301	96101
96407	96607	96207	96007	96439	96639	96239	96039	96471	96671	96271	96071	96503	96703	96303	96103
96409	96609	96209	96009	96441	96641	96241	96041	96473	96673	96273	96073	96505	96705	96305	96105
96411	96611	96211	96011	96443	96643	96243	96043	96475	96675	96275	96075	96507	96707	96307	96107
96413	96613	96213	96013	96445	96645	96245	96045	96477	96677	96277	96077	96509	96709	96309	96109
96415	96615	96215	96015	96447	96647	96247	96047	96479	96679	96279	96079	96511	96711	96311	96111
96417	96617	96217	96017	96449	96649	96249	96049	96481	96681	96281	96081	96513	96713	96313	96113
96419	96619	96219	96019	96451	96651	96251	96051	96483	96683	96283	96083	96515	96715	96315	96115
96421	96621	96221	96021	96453	96653	96253	96053	96485	96685	96285	96085	96517	96717	96317	96117
96423	96623	96223	96023	96455	96655	96255	96055	96487	96687	96287	96087	96519	96719	96319	96119
96425	96625	96225	96025	96457	96657	96257	96057	96489	96689	96289	96089	96521	96721	96321	96121
96427	96627	96227	96027	96459	96659	96259	96059	96491	96691	96291	96091	96523	96723	96323	96123
96429	96629	96229	96029	96461	96661	96261	96061	96493	96693	96293	96093	96525	96725	96325	96125
96431	96631	96231	96031	96463	96663	96263	96063	96495	96695	96295	96095				

2009 STOCK

Size of stock: Tube
Year of manufacture: 2006-2011
Built by: Bombardier Transportation
Entry into service: 2009
Lines used on: Victoria
Number of cars per train: 8
Train formation: DM-T-NDM-UNDM+UNDM-NDM-T-DM

Led by 11071, a Brixton bound service arrives at Warren Street, 18 January 2014.

The 2009 Stock first appeared on the London Underground in 2007, when a pre-production train underwent testing on the Victoria Line. A second pre-production train then entered passenger service in July 2009. The 2009 Stock is a close relative of the S Stock, both technically and also in looks. The trains were built to replace the 1967 Stock trains that had operated all Victoria Line services since its opening in the late 1960s. Enough of the production trains had entered service by 2011 for the 1967 Stock to be eradicated, and the last 1967 Stock ran in passenger service on 30 June 2011.

The 2009 Stock is 40mm wider than the 1967 Stock that they replaced. When the Victoria Line was built, the overall size of the tunnel bores was built to a slightly larger diameter than on previous lines, and so the 2009 Stock has been able to take advantage of this size, and with a thinner body shell, and externally hung doors, there is much more room inside the trains. This has allowed more room for standing passengers and also made it easier for the train to be accessed by wheelchairs and pushchairs. Due to their larger overall size, the trains cannot leave the Victoria Line by rail. The Victoria Line is connected to the rest of the Underground via the Piccadilly Line at Finsbury Park, but the trains are too large to fit in the Piccadilly Line tube tunnels, so if they leave the line, it must be by road.

The trains are operated automatically using the Invensys 'Distance to Go – Radio' (DTG-R) system of ATO/ATP. The Victoria Line has always been an automatic railway ever since opening, but the current

2009 Stock *to* Engineering Trains

system is more advanced than the system used by the 1967 Stock. As there was a period of changeover between the 1967 Stock and the 2009 Stock, the DTG-R system had to work alongside the previous system until the old stock had been withdrawn.

Internally, the trains are well equipped for carrying passengers with impaired mobility, with tip up seats that create space for wheelchairs and pushchairs, and the grab poles in the doorways are offset to allow enough room for a wheelchair to pass through easily. Lighting at floor level by each door, which is illuminated whenever the doors are opened, is also an aid to any passenger with a visual impairment.

2009 Stock (Victoria line)
8-car units

DM (D)	T	NDM	UNDM	UNDM	NDM	T	DM(A)	DM (D)	T	NDM	UNDM	UNDM	NDM	T	DM(A)
11001	12001	13001	14001	14002	13002	12002	11002	11049	12049	13049	14049	14050	13050	12050	11050
11003	12003	13003	14003	14004	13004	12004	11004	11051	12051	13051	14051	14052	13052	12052	11052
11005	12005	13005	14005	14006	13006	12006	11006	11053	12053	13053	14053	14054	13054	12054	11054
11007	12007	13007	14007	14008	13008	12008	11008	11055	12055	13055	14055	14056	13056	12056	11056
11009	12009	13009	14009	14010	13010	12010	11010	11057	12057	13057	14057	14058	13058	12058	11058
11011	12011	13011	14011	14012	13012	12012	11012	11059	12059	13059	14059	14060	13060	12060	11060
11013	12013	13013	14013	14014	13014	12014	11014	11061	12061	13061	14061	14062	13062	12062	11062
11015	12015	13015	14015	14016	13016	12016	11016	11063	12063	13063	14063	14064	13064	12064	11064
11017	12017	13017	14017	14018	13018	12018	11018	11065	12065	13065	14065	14066	13066	12066	11066
11019	12019	13019	14019	14020	13020	12020	11020	11067	12067	13067	14067	14068	13068	12068	11068
11021	12021	13021	14021	14022	13022	12022	11022	11069	12069	13069	14069	14070	13070	12070	11070
11023	12023	13023	14023	14024	13024	12024	11024	11071	12071	13071	14071	14072	13072	12072	11072
11025	12025	13025	14025	14026	13026	12026	11026	11073	12073	13073	14073	14074	13074	12074	11074
11027	12027	13027	14027	14028	13028	12028	11028	11075	12075	13075	14075	14076	13076	12076	11076
11029	12029	13029	14029	14030	13030	12030	11030	11077	12077	13077	14077	14078	13078	12078	11078
11031	12031	13031	14031	14032	13032	12032	11032	11079	12079	13079	14079	14080	13080	12080	11080
11033	12033	13033	14033	14034	13034	12034	11034	11081	12081	13081	14081	14082	13082	12082	11082
11035	12035	13035	14035	14036	13036	12036	11036	11083	12083	13083	14083	14084	13084	12084	11084
11037	12037	13037	14037	14038	13038	12038	11038	11085	12085	13085	14085	14086	13086	12086	11086
11039	12039	13039	14039	14040	13040	12040	11040	11087	12087	13087	14087	14088	13088	12088	11088
11041	12041	13041	14041	14042	13042	12042	11042	11089	12089	13089	14089	14090	13090	12090	11090
11043	12043	13043	14043	14044	13044	12044	11044	11091	12091	13091	14091	14092	13092	12092	11092
11045	12045	13045	14045	14046	13046	12046	11046	11093	12093	13093	14093	14094	13094	12094	11094
11047	12047	13047	14047	14048	13048	12048	11048								

ENGINEERING TRAINS

Every night, the London Underground shuts down for a period of about 4-5 hours. This period is used to perform a whole host of routine maintenance, inspections, engineering tasks, cleaning, changing adverts, station refurbishments etc… If and when the Night Tube is introduced, this will only apply to Friday and Saturday nights on selected lines, leaving all other nights of the week still available to the engineers, maintenance and cleaning staff.

Some tasks can be performed by a team in a van turning up at a location and carrying out their allotted tasks, but some jobs require the use of special trains, or they require large and heavy equipment and materials to be delivered by train. For this purpose, the London Underground has a fleet of engineering vehicles that many of the travelling public will rarely see. Some of these trains are specially built for the tasks that they perform, while others are converted from redundant stock in order to perform a specific task.

In addition to the overnight maintenance work, there are also some larger engineering tasks undertaken over longer periods, usually weekends, when sections of line are closed while track replacement, re-signalling, drainage work and other major tasks are undertaken. These often involve LU's own vehicles, but on the sub-surface network, can also involve trains that come in from Network Rail. While inconvenient for the traveller, these shut downs are aimed at improving the Underground network and represent a welcome investment in the infrastructure.

Engineering Trains

Battery Locomotives

Forming the backbone of the engineering fleet are 29 battery locomotives, which are used to haul engineering trains around the system. Although referred to as battery locomotives, they are in fact battery-electric locomotives, as they can operate as an electric locomotive drawing power from the conductor rails, but can also operate by taking power from the 320V onboard batteries. The usual method of operation is to travel to the worksite on electric power, but once at the worksite, the power is switched off, and the loco performs any movements using battery power. The locomotives are all built to an almost identical design, but were built in three batches by two different manufacturers. The oldest are L20-L32 that were built by Metro-Cammell in Birmingham in 1964/65. The next batch to be built were L15-L19, also built by Metro-Cammell in 1969/1970. Finally, L44-L54 were built by BREL Doncaster in 1973/74. All locomotives are to tube gauge. All of the fleet are fitted with tripcocks for use on lines with colour light signalling and trains stops, but several are also fitted with the Central Line ATP system and / or the TBTC system used on the Jubilee and Northern lines. No locos have yet been fitted with the Victoria Line DTG-R system, and any engineering train going onto the Victoria Line has to do so once there are no other trains moving on the line.

Like most other Underground trains, the battery locos have an 'A' end and a 'D' end. Four of the BREL locomotives (L50-L53) have had their buffers and screw / buckeye couplings removed from their 'A' end. This is to facilitate their use on long welded rail trains where they would couple to the train using the Ward coupler on their 'A' end. This does not preclude their use on other engineering trains, as they can still be used on other trains provided that the 'D' end is coupled to the train.

Engineering trains are usually top and tailed (i.e.: a loco on each end of the train). This makes reversing en route quick and easy, and also assists at the worksite itself as the train may need to be split in order to access equipment or materials being carried.

The battery loco fleet is currently undergoing life extension modifications. This involves fitting new batteries, revised cabs with the side doors plated over, and crew access moved to the door in the centre of the cab front. For safety reasons, railings are then fitted to the ends of the loco to make entering and exiting the cab through the centre door safe and easy. New, more powerful headlights and working lights have also been fitted to the ends of the locos. All locos are also being upgraded to work on 750V dc as well as 630V dc, as several lines are to have their power upgraded.

Battery loco L24 heads a Ruislip to Upminster Bridge train of rails through Sloane Square close to the end of traffic on 20 May 2015. This loco has received life extension modifications, and the new headlights and railings on the front of the loco can be clearly seen.

Engineering Trains

Schöma Locomotives

In 2000, Transplant inherited a fleet of 14 diesel locomotives that had been built for use on construction trains when the Jubilee Line Extension was being built. They were built by Schöma in 1995 with 500hp diesel engines fitted with exhaust scrubbers, which helps keep emissions down and allows their use in sub-surface tunnels (but not tube tunnels). At the end of 2014, two locomotives (2 and 5) were sent to Clayton Equipment in Burton-on-Trent for conversion into battery locomotives. Further locomotives have followed, and at the time of writing, only four diesel powered Schöma locos remained to be converted to battery locos (1, 3, 9 and 12). It is intended that the Schöma battery locos will operate in pairs alongside the existing battery loco fleet. Unlike the older battery locos, the Schömas can recharge their batteries while moving on electric power.

Schöma locomotive 5 is pictured at Wirksworth in Derbyshire while on test following conversion to a battery loco at Clayton Equipment in Burton on Trent. 14 February 2015.

Asset Inspection Train

Formed of a mix of 1967 Stock and 1972 MkI Stock vehicles, the AIT is intended for use monitoring track and other trackside equipment. The project to get this train into service was on hold for technical reasons at the time of writing, and it is not known when the train will enter service. It should eventually replace the Track Recording Train.

Track Recording Train

This train consists of two former 1960 Stock driving motors and a former 1973 Stock trailer car. It is used to travel around the Underground monitoring track condition, with the track recording equipment being housed in the trailer car. The train is tripcock fitted for use on conventionally signalled lines, and is also fitted with the Central Line's ATP system. It is not fitted with TBTC or DTG-R, and so any use on the Victoria, Jubilee and Northern lines has to be done under controlled conditions (a possession), and this usually takes place outside of traffic hours.

Engineering Trains

Unusually, the Track Recording Car is fitted with buckeye couplers at a height that makes them compatible with trains on Network Rail, thus allowing the trailer car to be hauled over Network Rail if needed. The cab ends of the 1960 Stock DMs have standard tube height drawgear.

The Track Recording Train formed of L132+TRC+TRC666+L133 passes through Kilburn Park on the Bakerloo Line on 25 November 2015.

Rail Adhesion Trains

The autumn leaf fall season causes problems at both ends of the Central Line and the north end of the Metropolitan Line. Wet leaves that are crushed by the weight of a train are turned into a dangerous slimy substance that can cause trains to slip when accelerating and skid when trying to stop. To help combat this, the Underground has some Rail Adhesion Trains (RATs) that apply a sticky

The Central Line's east end Rail Adhesion Train led by 1406 passes through a misty Snaresbrook while working a Hainault Depot – Leytonstone – Epping – Leytonstone – Woodford – Newbury Park – Hainault Depot circuit on 1 November 2015.

73

Engineering Trains

paste known as Sandite to the railhead to improve adhesion. These trains only operate during the autumn, usually the start of October through until December. The two Central Line trains are formed of 1962 Stock cars (and one 1959 Stock car). A 5-car train works at the west end of the Central between West Ruislip, White City and Ealing Broadway, and an 8-car train operates at the east end of the Central between Newbury Park, Hainault, Woodford, Leytonstone and Epping. On the Metropolitan Line, a 4-car train of A Stock, into which Rail Adhesion Car 6036 is inserted (making 5-cars), operates between Neasden Depot, Uxbridge, Watford, Chesham and Amersham. It is likely that the A Stock RAT may have worked its last duties during 2015, as a new RAT is being converted from redundant D Stock. It remains to be seen whether this will be ready in time to replace the A Stock in autumn 2016.

Track Maintenance Machines

Transplant has three tube gauge track maintenance machines (TMM771-TMM773) built in 1980 by Plasser & Theurer, and one full size points and crossings machine (TMM774) built by Franz Plasser in 2007. Two new machines were delivered from Matisa at the start of 2016. These are numbered TMM775 and TMM776 and are both to full loading gauge.

Rail Grinders and Rail Millers

Used for correcting the profile of the railhead, these machines are owned by contractors such as Schweerbau and Speno and are not part of the Transplant fleet.

Non-powered Vehicles

There is a large fleet of wagons available for forming into engineering trains in order to perform a variety of tasks. These include ballast hoppers, general purpose wagons, rail carriers, spoil and ballast wagons, flat wagons, drum wagons, well wagons and cranes. Some vehicles have been adapted for specific roles, while others are for general use.

Engineering Train Workings

Engineering trains, and the battery locomotives in particular, are of great interest to a lot of London Underground enthusiasts. While they hide away for most of the day and only come out at night, they can be seen in action with a little bit of effort.

The engineering fleet is based at Ruislip Depot at the west end of the Central Line. Any engineering trains that need to reach a location on the Central Line can depart eastwards onto the Central Line, emerging via the depot connection close to Ruislip Gardens station. To reach any other part of the Underground network (with the exception of the Waterloo & City Line which is isolated from the rest of the Underground network), trains can depart Ruislip Depot via Ruislip Siding which gives access to the Uxbridge branch of the Metropolitan and Piccadilly lines. From here, trains can head west towards Uxbridge, or head east towards Rayners Lane. Here there is a junction where the Metropolitan Line goes left towards Harrow-on-the-Hill and the Piccadilly Line goes right towards Ealing Common.

Turning left towards Harrow-on-the-Hill will allow trains to reach anywhere on the sub-surface network, and also the Jubilee Line via a connection at Neasden. Access to the Bakerloo Line is also via this route, as a Bakerloo bound engineering train would run via the Jubilee Line to Baker Street where it would cross over to the Bakerloo Line.

Turning right towards Ealing Common will also allow anywhere on the sub-surface network to be reached, and also anywhere on the Piccadilly Line. Trains heading to the Northern Line travel along the Piccadilly Line as far as King's Cross St Pancras where they reverse and then take a short curve

Engineering Trains

Battery Locomotives

L15 (Metro-Cammell 1970)	L30 (Metro-Cammell 1965)*
L16 (Metro-Cammell 1970)	L31 (Metro-Cammell 1965)*
L17 (Metro-Cammell 1970)*	L32 (Metro-Cammell 1965)*
L18 (Metro-Cammell 1970)*	L44 (BREL Doncaster 1974)*
L19 (Metro-Cammell 1970)	L45 (BREL Doncaster 1974)
L20 (Metro-Cammell 1964)	L46 (BREL Doncaster 1974)*
L21 (Metro-Cammell 1964)	L47 (BREL Doncaster 1974)
L22 (Metro-Cammell 1965)*	L48 (BREL Doncaster 1974)
L23 (Metro-Cammell 1965)*	L49 (BREL Doncaster 1974)*
L24 (Metro-Cammell 1965)*	L50 (BREL Doncaster 1974)**
L25 (Metro-Cammell 1965)*	L51 (BREL Doncaster 1974)*
L26 (Metro-Cammell 1965)*	L52 (BREL Doncaster 1974)
L27 (Metro-Cammell 1965)*	L53 (BREL Doncaster 1974)**
L28 (Metro-Cammell 1965)*	L54 (BREL Doncaster 1974)
L29 (Metro-Cammell 1965)*	

*Refurbished with modified cab ends
** Undergoing refurbishment at the time of going to press

Schoma Diesel Locomotives

1	Britta Lotta	8	Emma*
2	Nikki*	9	Debora
3	Claire	10	Clementine*
4	Pam*	11	Joan*
5	Sophie*	12	Melanie
6	Denise*	13	Michele*
7	Annemarie*	14	Carol*

*Converted to battery power

General Purpose Wagons (ex JLE)

JLE1	JLE3	JLE5	JLE7	JLE9	JLE11	JLE13
JLE2	JLE4	JLE6	JLE8	JLE10	JLE12	JLE14
						JLE15

General Purpose Wagons

GP901	GP909	GP917	GP925	GP933	GP941
GP902	GP910	GP918	GP926	GP934	
GP903	GP911	GP919	GP927	GP935	
GP904	GP912	GP920	GP928	GP936	
GP905	GP913	GP921	GP929	GP937	
GP906	GP914	GP922	GP930	GP938	
GP907	GP915	GP923	GP931	GP939	
GP908	GP916	GP924	GP932	GP940	

Match Wagons

MW956	MW957	MW958	MW959	MW960	MW961

Spoil and Ballast Wagons (ex BR Turbot)

SB231	SB240	SB249	SB258	SB267	SB276	SB285
SB232	SB241	SB250	SB259	SB268	SB277	SB286
SB233	SB242	SB251	SB260	SB269	SB278	SB287
SB234	SB243	SB252	SB261	SB270	SB279	SB288
SB235	SB244	SB253	SB262	SB271	SB280	SB289
SB236	SB245	SB254	SB263	SB272	SB281	SB290
SB237	SB246	SB255	SB264	SB273	SB282	
SB238	SB247	SB256	SB265	SB274	SB283	
SB239	SB248	SB257	SB266	SB275	SB284	

Hopper Wagons

HW201	HW204	HW207	HW210	HW213	HW216	HW219
HW202	HW205	HW208	HW211	HW214	HW217	HW220
HW203	HW206	HW209	HW212	HW215	HW218	HW221
						HW222

Bogie Well Wagon (ex JLE)

JLE16	JLE17	JLE18
		JLE19

Cable Drum Wagon (ex JLE)

JLE20	JLE21	JLE22
		JLE23

Cement Mixer Wagons

CM950	CM952	CM954
CM951	CM953	CM955

Deep Well Cable Drum Wagon

CW1053	CW1054	CW1055

75

Engineering Trains

Rail Wagons

RW495	RW802	RW806	RW810	RW814	RW818	RW822
RW505	RW803	RW807	RW811	RW815	RW819	RW823
RW506	RW804	RW808	RW812	RW816	RW820	RW824
RW801	RW805	RW809	RW813	RW817	RW821	RW825
						RW826

High Deck Wagons

HD871	HD872	HD873	HD874	HD875	HD876

Track Maintenance Machines

TMM771	Plasser Theurer 1980	
TMM772	Plasser Theurer 1980	
TMM773	Plasser Theurer 1980	Named 'Alan Jenkins'
TMM774	Franz Plasser 2007	
TMM775	Matisa 2016	
TMM776	Matisa 2016	

Note: TMM771-773 are tube size TMM774-776 are full size

Diesel Hydraulic Crane

C623	C624	C625	C626

Diesel Hydraulic Crane (Twin Jib)

TRM627	TRM628

1972 MkI Stock / 1967 Stock* Asset Inspection Train

DM(A)	T	DM(D)	DM(A)	T	DM(D)
3213	4213	3179*	3079*	4313	3313

Track Recording Train

L132	Ex 1960 Stock DM 3901
TRC666	Ex 1973 Stock trailer 514
L133	Ex 1960 Stock DM 3905

D Stock (for conversion to Rail Adhesion Train)

DM	UNDM	T	UNDM	DM
7010	8123	17010	8010	7123

A60/A62 Stock

DM(A)	T	T	DM(D)	Notes
5110	6110	6111	5111	
5112	6112	6113	5113	Acton Works (spare)
5234	6234	6235	5235	
	6036			Rail Adhesion Car
	6132			Acton Works (stored)

1973 Stock

T	DM(D)	Notes
566	366	Northfields

1967 Stock

DM(A)	T	T	DM(D)	Notes
3060	4060	4160	3160	Acton Works
3061	4061	4161	3161	Acton Works
3067	4067	4167	3167	London Road (ambience training vehicles)
3075	4075	4175	3175	Acton Works
3022			3122	Acton Works
3007			3107	Acton Works

1972 MkI/MkII Stock

DM(A)	T	T	DM(D)	UNDM	Notes
3202	4202	4302	3302		Acton Works (used for shunting)
	4511			3411	Hainault depot (stored)
3229	4229	4329	3329		Aldwych

1962 Stock (*1959 tock)

DM(A)	T	NDM	DM(D)	DM(A)	T	NDM	NDM	T	DM(D)	Notes
1406	2682	9125*	1681	1682		9577		2406	1407	8-car Sandite 1
1570		9691			2440		9441		1441	5-car Sandite 2
1690	9459**		1691							Acton Works (Spare)

** = Former NDM, currently a trailer (without motors)

Engineering Trains

called the King's Cross loop which emerges onto the Northern Line close to Euston (Bank branch). Trains can then proceed northbound up the Northern Line through Euston towards Camden Town and beyond, or they can cross over via the Euston loop into the southbound platform, where they can reverse and head south down the Bank branch of the Northern Line. Trains heading to the Victoria Line will also travel along the Piccadilly Line as far as Finsbury Park where they can cross over onto the Victoria Line.

In order for engineering trains to reach their worksites and allow enough time for work to be carried out, they need to arrive as close behind the last train as possible. For this reason, trains often leave Ruislip Depot well before the end of traffic in the Ruislip / Rayners Lane area (usually from any time around 2300 onwards), and can be easily seen by any late night travellers. In the morning, the reverse happens, and trains usually leave the worksite just ahead of the first passenger train of the day, and can take a little while to get back to Ruislip and can often be seen by early morning travellers. Weekend engineering jobs often see a procession of trains leaving Ruislip on a Friday night, some of which may well return during daytime during the course of the weekend, although these are very unpredictable.

Engineering trains run as required, and although they can run on any night, the majority of trains involved in overnight engineering leave Ruislip on Monday to Thursday nights, returning on Tuesday to Friday mornings. If you are travelling on the Underground late at night or early in the mornings on these days, especially around Ealing Common, Harrow-on-the-Hill, Rayners Lane, Ruislip area, you are very likely to see them.

L21 is seen on the rear of a weekend possession train heading for Kilburn as it passes eastbound through Ruislip Manor on 3 April 2015. This train passed through here at 0116 (the last train to call at this station was due at 0123 in the westbound direction).

The 1972 MkI set (3329-4329-4229-3229) that is kept at Aldwych for filming and training purposes, is seen passing through Barons Court on its way to Northfields Depot for inspection and maintenance. This journey was made just ahead of the first Piccadilly Line service of the day, 21 March 2015.

77

Heritage Operations

HERITAGE OPERATIONS

Although the London Underground's main reason for existence is to move millions of people around London, it has always recognised the history that brought it to where it is today. This is very apparent in many of the stations, quite a few of which have been sympathetically restored, and some are even listed buildings. The London Transport Museum in Covent Garden is well worth a visit and includes items covering not just the Underground, but also other transport items such as buses and trams. Not everything that the LTM owns can be accommodated at Covent Garden, and they also have a large storage depot at Acton which stages occasional open days (usually 2-3 per year). The store can also be visited by appointment – see the London Transport Museum for details (www.ltmuseum.co.uk).

In conjunction with Transport for London, the London Transport Museum occasionally operates special heritage trains on parts of the Underground network. At the time of writing, none were planned, but in 2015, there was a weekend of steam operation between Watford and Chesham to celebrate 90 years of the Watford branch. Details of any forthcoming heritage train trips are usually advertised on the London Transport Museum website.

Stock that may be used on heritage trains trips are as follows:

1938 Tube Stock – 10012-012256-12048-11012 (currently under repair at Acton Works)
Metropolitan Vickers Electric locomotive number 12 'Sarah Siddons'
Ex BR 4TC set – 70823, 71163, 76297 and 76324
Ex GWR 'Prairie' tank L150 (GWR 5521 – hired in as required)
Metropolitan Railway 'E' class No.1 (hired in as required)
Metropolitan Ashbury's coaches 368, 387, 394 and 412 (hired in)
Metropolitan Railway milk van No.4
Metropolitan Railway 'Jubilee' coach 353

During the Watford 90 specials, Metropolitan Railway 'E' class No.1 leads electric loco number 12 'Sarah Siddons' along the Chesham branch at Quill Hall Farm on 12 September 2015. The train is formed of 'Jubilee' coach 353, the four Ashbury's coaches (often referred to as 'The Chesham Set'), milk van number 4, and Ex GWR 'Prairie' tank 5521, which is disguised in London Transport livery as L150.

A to Z

A to Z OF UNDERGROUND STATIONS

Acton Town ● District ● Piccadilly (zone 3)

Acton Town is a busy four platform station served by both the District and Piccadilly lines. Opened in July 1879, Acton Town was originally named Mill Hill Park and was served initially by the Metropolitan District Railway's Ealing Broadway branch. The name was changed to Acton Town in 1910. At street level, the station has a fine example of a Charles Holden designed 'brick box with concrete lid' station building which dates from 1932. To the west of the station lies the junction where the Piccadilly's Heathrow branch diverges away from the Ealing Broadway and the Uxbridge branches of the District and Piccadilly. Adjacent to this junction are the District's Ealing Common depot and the Acton store of the London Transport Museum (which holds a small number of open days per year and is well worth a visit). At one time, Acton Town had a fifth platform, which is still there, minus track, and mostly hidden by advertising boards opposite platform 4. This platform served a short branch to South Acton and was operated by a single motor car. The branch opened in 1905 and was closed in 1959.

At the east end of the station there are three reversing sidings situated between the westbound and eastbound tracks. On the south side of the line at this point is London Underground's Acton Works, which is accessed via a connection with the westbound local adjacent to platform 1.

The 2225 Uxbridge to Oakwood Piccadilly Line service arrives at Acton Town's platform 3 on 19 May 2015. For most of the day, Piccadilly Line trains run non-stop between Acton Town and Hammersmith, but early morning and late at night, trains will also call at Turnham Green.

Aldgate ● Circle ● Metropolitan (zone 1)

Opened in November 1876, Aldgate is situated in a triangle of lines at the eastern edge of the Circle Line. Aldgate has four platforms made up of two platform islands, the outer faces of which are served exclusively by the Circle Line (outer rail platform 1, and inner rail platform 4). The two centre tracks which serve platforms 2 and 3 are dead end roads which form the City terminus of the Metropolitan Line. Immediately to the north of the platforms is Aldgate North Junction where Hammersmith & City Line trains leave the inner circle and head to Aldgate East and on to Barking. At the south end of the station is Minories Junction where the District Line leaves the inner circle to head to Aldgate East, where it is joined by the Hammersmith & City Line from Aldgate North Junction. This makes Aldgate the only station from which you can see trains from all four of the sub-surface lines.

Aldgate East ● District ● Hammersmith & City (zone 1)

The original station at Aldgate East was opened in October 1884 as part of the Metropolitan District Railway's extension to Whitechapel, but this station closed on 30 October 1938 and was replaced by the current station which opened the following day. The reason for re-siting the station was to allow the enlargement of the Aldgate triangle as part of the '1935-40 New Works Programme'. The new station, being further to the east than the original, was close enough to the next station at St Mary's, that this station was closed on the same day that the original Aldgate East station closed.

A to Z Alperton *to* Arnos Grove

Alperton ● Piccadilly (zone 4)
Located on the Piccadilly's Uxbridge branch, Alperton was opened by the Metropolitan District Railway as Perivale Alperton on 28 June 1903, being renamed Alperton in 1910. The station building is a Charles Holden brick, reinforced concrete and glass affair dating from 1931 and is situated at street level, with the platforms and track being high above the street. At one time, Alperton had an escalator up to the eastbound platform, one of only two stations to have an escalator up to platform level (the other being Greenford on the Central Line). This escalator is no longer in use and is not visible, being located behind a brick wall.

Amersham ● Metropolitan (zone 9)
Opened by the Metropolitan Railway on 1 September 1892 as part of that railway's extension from Chalfont & Latimer to Aylesbury, Amersham is today a terminus for Metropolitan Line trains. The tracks continue beyond Amersham, minus conductor rails, and this is served by Chiltern Railway's trains which operate between London Marylebone and Aylesbury, which also call at Amersham. The boundary between London Underground and Network Rail is to the west of Amersham at Mantles Wood. Metropolitan Line trains usually arrive at Amersham and proceed into one of two sidings to reverse. Although Chesham station is the most westerly location that passengers can travel to on the Underground, the sidings at Amersham are very slightly further west than Chesham station and therefore they are the most westerly point on the Underground.

Angel ● Northern (zone 1)
Until the 1990s, both the southbound and northbound tracks at Angel were in one tunnel and served by a central island platform, a layout typical of the City & South London Railway, and an arrangement that still exists today at Clapham North and Clapham Common. As part of an upgrade in the 90s, the northbound track was diverted into a new platform tunnel, and the space that it used to occupy, in what is now the southbound tunnel, was filled in to create an extra wide platform. Angel station was opened on 17 November 1901 as the northern terminus of the City & South London Railway's extension from Moorgate Street. It became a through station when this line was further extended beyond Angel to Euston on 12 May 1907.

Archway ● Northern (zones 2 and 3)
Opened by the Charing Cross, Euston & Hampstead Railway on 22 June 1907 as Highgate, this station was originally a terminus station. It became a through station from 3 July 1939 when the line was extended to join the LNER at East Finchley. It was renamed Highgate (Archway) when the current Highgate station (the next station towards East Finchley) opened on 19 January 1941, and then became just Archway in 1947. To the north of the platforms there is a centre reversing siding to turn northbound trains back south. This is only used at times of service disruption.

Arnos Grove ● Piccadilly (zone 4)
The station building here consists of a cylindrical version of Charles Holden's 'brick box with concrete lid' and dates from the opening of the Piccadilly Line's Cockfosters extension, opening on 19 September 1932. It performed the role of a terminus until the next stage of the extension opened to Oakwood on 13 March 1933. There are three tracks through the station, the centre track having a platform face on both sides, and used mostly by trains that are timetabled to reverse here, although it can also be used as a through road. To the south of the station, there are seven sidings that are used to stable trains outside of traffic hours.

A to Z Arsenal *to* Baker Street

Arsenal 🔵 Piccadilly (zone 2)
This is the only station on the London Underground to be named after a football club, but it was originally called Gillespie Road, and replica tiles on the platforms still display this name. The station was renamed Arsenal (Highbury Hill) in 1932, and then to just Arsenal sometime around 1960. There are no lifts or escalators at this station, instead, access to the platforms is via a sloping walkway from the entrance.

Baker Street 🟣 Metropolitan 🟡 Circle 🩷 Hammersmith & City 🟤 Bakerloo ⚪ Jubilee (zone 1)
The Baker Street station complex has ten platforms, the oldest of which are platforms 5 and 6 which serve the Circle & Hammersmith & City lines and which date from the opening of the world's first underground railway which opened in January 1863 between Paddington (Bishop's Road) and Farringdon Street. Platforms 5 and 6 are situated beneath a brick arch roof which dates back to the line's opening and is in as near original condition as modern operations will allow. Alongside to the north of the original platforms are four platforms (1 to 4) that are served by the Metropolitan Line. Platforms 1 and 4 are dead end roads used by trains from the north that terminate here and platforms 2 and 3 are through platforms served by Metropolitan trains to and from Aldgate. Just beyond the south end of these platforms, and to the east of platforms 5 and 6, the Metropolitan Line and the Circle and Hammersmith & City lines join together at Baker Street Junction.

Platforms 8 and 9 are served by the Bakerloo Line, and the platform walls are decorated with silhouettes of the fictional character Sherlock Holmes, who supposedly lived at 221b Baker Street. Look closely at these silhouettes and you will find that they are made up of lots of tiny Sherlock Holmes silhouettes.

On 20 November 1939, a new twin track tunnel section was opened between Finchley Road and a new junction with the Bakerloo Line at Baker Street. This allowed the Bakerloo to take over the Stanmore branch from the Metropolitan. In the southbound direction, trains from the Watford Junction and Stanmore branches each had their own separate platforms, but northbound trains to both branches had to share the current northbound Bakerloo platform which created a bottleneck. A new line to be known as the Jubilee Line, was constructed between Baker Street and Charing

The glorious platforms 5 and 6 at Baker Street with a train of S Stock led by 21472 arriving into platform 5 with a Hammersmith & City Line service for Barking on 30 July 2015.

Cross which included a new northbound platform at Baker Street. This new line opened on 1 May 1979 and also included the transfer of the Bakerloo's Stanmore branch to the Jubilee. Today there is interchange between the lines for passengers, but the physical junction between the two lines only sees occasional use, mostly by engineering trains between Ruislip Depot and the Bakerloo.

Balham ● Northern (zone 3)

Situated on the Morden extension, in common with the other stations on this extension, Balham has a Portland Stone Charles Holden designed station building. This station was the scene of a tragic incident during World War II, when a bomb landed on the road above. A bus crashed into the crater and the platform tunnel partly collapsed and was also filled with water from a broken water main. 60 people lost their lives and a memorial plaque is located in the ticket hall.

Bank ○ Waterloo & City ● Northern ● Central ● District ● Circle (zone 1)

There are no station buildings above ground, but sitting on top of a ventilation shaft on a plinth in front of the Royal Exchange is a statue of James Henry Greathead (see picture on the next page), the inventor of the Greathead Shield, a method by which early tube tunnels were bored through the ground. Below ground, located in a passageway that leads to the Waterloo & City Line, a section of a Greathead Shield can be found forming a part of the foot tunnel (below). This was in the former W&C siding tunnel and was found when the subway from the W&C to the Northern and DLR was being built.

This station is a large Underground complex which not only links the Waterloo & City, Northern and Central Lines, but also the Docklands Light Railway. The nearby Monument station is also connected below ground to the Bank complex, which provides interchange with the District and Circle lines as well. It is said that to walk through all of the foot tunnels within the complex would take well over an hour. There are currently construction works taking place to increase further the capacity of the Bank / Monument complex.

The Central Line platforms are on a sharp curve here as they follow the roads above, the westbound platform (5) being a continuous curve, while the eastbound platform (6) has a short straight section at its east end. To the east of the station, the Central Line tracks also swerve to avoid the vaults of the Bank of England.

A to Z   Barbican *to* Barking

The Waterloo & City Line only has only two stations (Waterloo and Bank). The Bank end of the route consists of two terminal platforms (7 and 8), both of which see use, but at peak times, just one platform is scheduled to be used in order to prevent Train Operators 'stepping back' from having to switch between platforms. As this line is used to ferry city workers between the mainline station at Waterloo and the City of London, it is usually closed on Sundays and Bank Holidays.

The Northern Line platforms are numbered 3 and 4 and the trains run on the right through here. Right hand running takes place from just south of Borough station, to just north of Bank station with the running tunnels rolling over each other at each location.

Platform numbers 1 and 2 are taken by the District and Circle lines at Monument, and platforms 9 and 10 form the Bank terminus of the Docklands Light Railway, platform 10 being set down only, and platform 9 being for boarding only (trains reverse in a siding beyond the platforms).

Barbican   ● Circle   ● Hammersmith & City   ● Metropolitan (zone 1)
Opened as part of the Metropolitan Railway's extension from Farringdon Street to Moorgate Street on 23 December 1865, Barbican was originally called Aldersgate Street. It became Barbican in 1968. Alongside the two platforms used by the Underground are two abandoned platforms that used to serve the former 'Widened Lines' to Moorgate, and which closed in December 2009. The station is just below street level and is flanked on either side by large retaining walls. These walls used to support a glass and steel overall roof, and close examination will reveal the brackets that held this roof in place are still attached to the walls. The overall roof was removed after being damaged in an air raid in December 1941. Until 2015, there was a (long-disused) signal cabin at the west end of the westbound platform, but this was removed as part of the Crossrail project.

Barking   ● District   ● Hammersmith & City (zone 4)
Barking has 8 platforms, with 4 of them being served by the Underground. There is interchange between the Underground and services on Network Rail operated by London Overground and C2C. All Hammersmith & City Line trains and selected District Line trains terminate here. H&C trains usually terminate via the sidings to the east of the station, while apart from one train, terminating District trains reverse in the bay platform. In order to avoid conflicting movements with Network Rail trains, and to provide easy cross platform interchange between Underground and Network Rail trains, the westbound Underground line approaches from the east via an underpass, and leaves to the west over a flyover. There is a physical link between Network Rail and the London Underground at the west end of platform 1a, and this sees occasional use by engineering trains coming onto the Underground from Network Rail outside of traffic hours.

A to Z Barkingside *to* Bayswater

Barkingside 🔴 Central (zone 4)
This station was opened by the Great Eastern Railway in 1903 as part of their Woodford to Ilford route. The station became a part of the Underground when the Central Line took over the route between Newbury Park and Woodford in May 1948. The station buildings are still in near original condition and are grade II listed. Things to look out for here are the letters GER which are cast into the platform canopy support brackets and the 'General Waiting Room' etched into the glass of the waiting room windows (below and right).

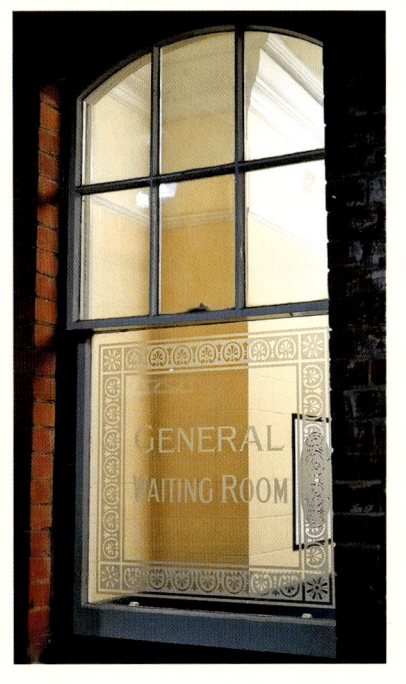

Barons Court 🟢 District 🔵 Piccadilly (zone 2)
The first railway through here was opened by the Metropolitan District Railway in September 1874, but the station was not built until 1905. It was built to serve new developments in the area and also to prepare for the coming of the Great Northern, Piccadilly & Brompton Railway which opened through here on 15 December 1906. There is cross platform interchange here between the Piccadilly and the District. To the east of Barons Court, the Piccadilly dives down into tube tunnel between the eastbound and westbound tracks of the District. Objects of interest here include the old style light box train describers and the Grade II listed station building designed by Harry Ford, which still bears the name 'District Railway' above the entrance.

Bayswater 🟡 Circle 🟢 District (zone 1)
This station retains its overall roof, although at platform level, there is very little of this roof to be seen. Girders span the tracks just above train height, and above this, the arch of the overall roof is used as a garage by a car hire firm. Just a short walk away from the station, in a street named Leinster Gardens, is a remarkable set of buildings. The line was built in the 1860s (opened in 1868) and was built by the very disruptive 'cut and cover' method. The line, being just below ground level, cut through the terrace on Leinster Gardens and necessitated the destruction of part of the terrace. Rather than leave a gaping hole, the Metropolitan Railway built a pair of dummy houses (pictured on the next page) to maintain the appearance of the terrace. The buildings are still there today, and from the front do not appear to look out of place, however, close examination will reveal that the doors and windows are painted on. Take a walk around the back into Porchester Terrace, and it can be clearly seen that the dummy houses (pictured next page) are nothing more than a 5m thick wall.

A to Z Becontree *to* Bermondsey

Becontree ● District (zone 5)
Opened in 1926 with the name Gale Street Halt, the station was rebuilt in 1932 to serve the two new tracks that were built by the LMS to serve the District. The name was changed to Becontree upon completion of this rebuild. Alongside the two District Line platforms are two disused platforms that used to serve the former London, Tilbury & Southend Railway tracks that the District runs parallel to here. These platforms were taken out of use in 1962 when the former LT&SR tracks (now part of Network Rail) were electrified.

Belsize Park ● Northern (zone 2)
With its fine Leslie Green designed red tiled building at street level, Belsize Park is on the Edgware branch of the Northern and was opened by the Charing Cross, Euston & Hampstead Railway on 22 June 1907. Immediately to the north of the platforms, the Edgware branch passes beneath the Network rail Midland Main Line.

Bermondsey ● Jubilee (zone 2)
Opened on 17 September 1999, Bermondsey is on the Jubilee Line Extension and does not connect with any other railway lines. In common with all the other JLE stations that are built below ground, Bermondsey is fitted with Platform Edge Doors (PEDs). The station was constructed as part tube and part cut and cover, and there is even a small chink of daylight that reaches the east end of the eastbound platform.

Descending to platform level at Bermondsey.

A to Z Bethnal Green *to* Bond Street

Bethnal Green 🔴 Central (zone 2)
The tragic events of 3 March 1943 will be long remembered in Bethnal Green where there was a terrible loss of life due to a freak accident. Work on an eastern extension of the Central Line was halted when war broke out, but the station at Bethnal Green was part completed and was put into use as an air raid shelter. On the date in question, it is believed that a new type of anti-aircraft rocket was launched from the nearby Victoria Park, the sound of which caused people to run to Bethnal Green station to take shelter, and in the panic that followed, a lady carrying a small child tripped and fell on the stairs. As more people tried to push their way into the station, approximately 300 people became trapped in the small stairwell and 173 people lost their lives, mostly through suffocation. A small plaque above one of the station entrances marks this event, but a larger memorial (called the Stairway to Heaven) is now in place near one of the entrances in the adjacent Bethnal Green Gardens.

Blackfriars 🟢 District 🟡 Circle (zone 1)
Located on the south side of the 'inner circle', Blackfriars has two platforms on the Underground and is served by trains on both the District and Circle lines. Interchange is also available here with the Network Rail station served by Thameslink and Southeastern services. The station underwent a major refurbishment in 2012.

Blackhorse Road 🔵 Victoria (zone 3)
The penultimate stop before the northern terminus of the Victoria at Walthamstow Central, Blackhorse Road gives interchange with the London Overground Gospel Oak to Barking service. The seat recesses here are decorated with a long black horse which also resembles a road.

Bond Street ⚪ Jubilee 🔴 Central (zone 1)
Opened as part of the Central London Railway's Shepherd's Bush to Bank line in 1900, Bond Street was served only by the Central until the opening of the Jubilee Line in 1979. Since then, the station has provided interchange between the two lines, as well as serving the busy shopping area above. In the future there will also be interchange here with Crossrail. Bond Street is the nearest station to the Selfridges department store, and in 1909, Harry Selfridge attempted to get the station name changed to 'Selfridges', but this was flatly refused by the CLR.

The main station entrance is through the West One shopping arcade on Oxford Street, which is located just west of the junction between Oxford Street and New Bond Street.

This picture clearly shows how the tracks descend upon departure from the Central Line eastbound platform at Bond Street. The practice of climbing into a station and then descending away from it uses gravity to assist deceleration and acceleration of trains, and is apparent at many (but not all) tube stations.

A to Z   Borough *to* Brent Cross

Borough ● Northern (zone 1)
To the south of the station, the northbound and southbound tunnels roll over each other so that trains run on the right. The tunnels roll back over to give left hand running again to the north of Bank station. Borough is the most northerly of the original City & South London Railway stations dating from 1890, as the next station north of here would have been the original terminus of the C&SLR at King William Street, which closed when the extension to Moorgate Street opened in February 1900.

Boston Manor ● Piccadilly (zone 4)
Opened by the Metropolitan District Rail as Boston Road on 1 May 1883, this station still retains the old District Railway signal cabin (actually a Saxby & Farmer designed and built cabin) which was in use from the line's opening in 1883 until 1905 when automatic signalling was introduced. Although not used for its original purpose for over a century, the signal cabin is kept in very good condition. At platform level, the station retains its District Railway platform buildings and canopies, but the street level entrance building and ticket hall dates from 1934 and was designed by Stanley Heaps. A good view of Northfields depot can be had from the opposite side of the road to the station entrance. Northfields depot has an entrance / exit at both ends, and trains entering or departing the depot at the west end pass behind the westbound platform (1) at Boston Manor. Trains that are shunting in the depot also sometimes come alongside Boston Manor station as there is a shunt neck located alongside the entrance / exit track.

Bounds Green ● Piccadilly (zones 3 and 4)
The station building here is of a style that is typical of the work of Charles Holden, but it is in fact the only station building on the Piccadilly Line Cockfosters extension that is not designed by him. It was in fact designed by Charles Holden's colleague C.H. James instead. Heading towards Cockfosters from Bounds Green, the line emerges into daylight between Bounds Green and Arnos Grove, the first time a train would have seen daylight since entering tube tunnel just east of Barons Court in West London. At the east end of the westbound platform, a small plaque commemorates the 16 Belgian refugees and 3 British citizens who died here on 13 October 1940, when part of the westbound platform tunnel collapsed, after houses above were hit and destroyed during an air raid.

Bow Road ● District ● Hammersmith & City (zone 2)
This is a very unusual station as the sub surface railway runs beneath the Bow Road to the west of this station, but emerges into daylight by curving away from the road in the station itself. This means that the west end of the station is in cut and cover tunnel, and the east end is in the open air. Interchange is available here with the Docklands Light Railway's Bow Church station, albeit with a 300 yard walk. Departing eastwards, trains face a climb of 1 in 32 up to Campbell Road Junction where the Underground's tracks come alongside the Network Rail lines in and out of Fenchurch Street (the former London, Tilbury & Southend Railway).

Brent Cross ● Northern (zone 3)
This station consists of an island platform on an elevated section of railway. The station building is at a lower level on the east side of the tracks and is a Stanley Heaps designed building fronted by a concrete roof supported by six sets of Doric columns. When opened on 19 November 1923, the station was just called Brent. It was renamed to Brent

Cross when the nearby Brent Cross shopping centre opened in 1976. It will be noted that the trackbed through the station is wide enough to accommodate two additional tracks, one on either side, where in the mid 1920s, a passing loop was added in each direction to allow faster trains to overtake slower ones. The loops did not last long and were removed in the 1930s. Immediately to the north of the station, a viaduct carries the line over the A406 North Circular Road and the River Brent.

Brixton 🔵 Victoria (zone 2)

The current southern terminus of the Victoria Line, Brixton opened on 23 July 1971 as part of an extension from Victoria. The station entrance is a modern glass fronted building which has a very large roundel mounted on the glass above the entrance. This is believed to be the largest London Underground roundel on the Underground system. There is interchange here with Network Rail's Brixton station via a very short walk. Below ground, the station is a two platform terminus with the running tunnels extending for a short distance beyond the south end of the platforms, where two trains stable outside of traffic hours. At the north end of the station there is a scissors crossover giving access to and from both platforms.

Bromley-by-Bow 🟢 District 🩷 Hammersmith & City (zones 2 and 3)

There are four tracks through Bromley-by-Bow, with the two tracks of the Underground running parallel to the two tracks of the former London, Tilbury & Southend Railway in and out of Fenchurch Street, now part of Network Rail and served by trains operated by C2C. The station was opened as Bromley by the LT&SR in 1858, and District Railway trains first called here in 1902 when trains were still steam hauled. Electrification and separation of the District tracks followed in 1905. From 1962, the platforms on the tracks in and out of Fenchurch Street were closed and the station has only been served by the Underground ever since. Although the platforms on the Network Rail tracks are still there, they are disused and not in good condition. The station building dates from 1972 and replaced the previous 1894 built building that was destroyed by a fire in 1970. The name of the station was changed to Bromley-by-Bow in 1967.

Buckhurst Hill 🔴 Central (zone 5)

Opened by the Eastern Counties Railway in 1856, this station became a part of the London Underground in November 1948 when the Central Line was extended eastwards over former LNER metals. The station building was built by the Great Eastern Railway and dates from 1892.

Burnt Oak ⚫ Northern (zone 4)

The first trains passed through here when the final section of the extension to Edgware was opened from Hendon Central on 18 August 1924, but the station here was not completed in time and did not open until 27 October 1924. The station building, designed by Stanley Heaps, was not completed until 1925. When opened, the station was called Burnt Oak (Watling), and became just Burnt Oak in the 1950s.

Caledonian Road 🔵 Piccadilly (zone 2)

With a superb Leslie Green designed grade II listed station building, this station dates back to the opening of the Great Northern, Piccadilly & Brompton Railway on 15 December 1906. At platform level, the station retains its unique tile colour scheme together with tiled station name and 'to Finsbury Park' and 'to Hammersmith' arrows on the platform tunnel walls. There are also 1908 style roundels on the end of each platform. Today, the next station on the westbound is King's Cross St Pancras, but when the line opened, the next station would have been York Road. This station closed in 1932, but it is still there, and just about visible from passing trains. The station is due to close for lift replacement from Spring 2016.

A to Z   Camden Town *to* Canary Wharf

Tiled station name and 1908 style roundel at Caledonian Road

Camden Town ● Northern (zone 2)
This station is a major hub on the Northern Line and today forms the junction of the Charing Cross and Bank branches to the south and the Edgware and High Barnet branches to the north. The station was opened by the Charing Cross, Euston & Hampstead Railway on 22 June 1907. Then it formed a junction where the Golders Green branch (since extended to Edgware) and the Highgate branch (since extended to High Barnet) split. On 20 April 1924, the City & South London Railway extension from Euston, and this connected the C&SLR to the CCE&HR at Camden Town. The entire junction is to the south of the platforms, and trains from either of the two branches through the city (via Charing Cross or via Bank) can reach both the Edgware and High Barnet branches and vice versa. Northbound trains go into platforms that are dedicated to whichever branch they are going on, with platform 1 being for the Edgware branch and platform 3 for the High Barnet branch. Southbound trains from the Edgware branch arrive into platform 2, but can go forward either via Bank or via Charing Cross, and southbound trains from the High Barnet branch arrive into platform 4, and again, can go forward via either of the branches through the city.

Canada Water ● Jubilee (zone 2)
Interchange is available here with London Overground (the former London Underground East London Line). At street level, the circular station building is a fine example of modern architecture, while at platform level, the station follows other below ground stations on the JLE in having platform edge doors.

Canary Wharf ● Jubilee (zone 2)
This station serves the busy Canary Wharf complex and has two glass domed entrances, one at each end of the station. Below ground, the station has very large proportions, being built to accommodate a very high volume of passengers. The platform is an island platform with platform edge doors on each platform face. A scissors crossover is located just beyond the west end of the platforms, and this can be used to reverse trains from either direction, although this is only normally used at times of service disruption. Interchange is available here with the Docklands Light Railway, either at the DLR's Canary Wharf station, or the nearby Heron Quays station.

A to Z Canning Town *to* Chalk Farm

Canning Town ● Jubilee (zone 2)
The Jubilee Line Extension, having just emerged into daylight arrives at Canning Town station. Here there is interchange with the Docklands Light Railway and numerous bus services that call at the adjacent bus station. The station is on the site of the former Thames Iron Works, and a concrete plaque pays homage to the site's previous incarnation. On top of this plaque is a slab of iron from HMS Warrior, the world's first all iron armour plated battleship. This ship still survives and has been fully restored and is based in Portsmouth.

Cannon Street ● District ● Circle (zone 1)
Opened by the Metropolitan District Railway on 6 October 1884, Cannon Street sub-surface station is located immediately beneath the Cannon Street mainline terminus. There are two platforms, platform 1 serves the westbound District and outer rail Circle, and platform 2 serves

the eastbound District and inner Rail Circle. Interchange is available here between the Underground and the mainline terminus above.

Canons Park ● Jubilee (zone 5)
Opened with the Metropolitan Railway's Stanmore branch as Canons Park (Edgware) on 10 December 1932, the station became just Canons Park in 1933. Now a station on the Jubilee Line, the station is atop an embankment, with entrances to the station beneath the overbridge where the railway crosses over the B461 Whitchurch Lane, close to the entrance to 'The Hive' stadium, home of Barnet Football Club and the London Broncos Rugby League Club. The stadium is clearly visible from passing Jubilee Line trains to the south of Canons Park station.

Chalfont & Latimer ● Metropolitan (zone 8)
Located in Little Chalfont, this station opened as Chalfont Road when the Metropolitan Railway opened its extension beyond Rickmansworth to Chesham on 8 July 1889. It became a junction station when a further extension was opened towards Aylesbury on 1 September 1892. The station name was changed to Chalfont & Latimer in 1915.

The station today has three platforms, with platform 1 being northbound, and platform 2 being southbound. Platform 3 is a bay platform that was used by Chesham services when the branch was worked as a shuttle between Chalfont & Latimer and Chesham. This method of operation ceased with the introduction of the S Stock, as the S Stock trains are too long to fit in the bay platform, the shuttle having been operated by a 4-car A Stock unit prior to the demise of this type of stock on the Underground. The bay is now occasionally used to stable engineering vehicles. Services on the Chesham branch now operate to and from London. Of note here are the co-acting colour light signals at the start of the Chesham branch. As well as Metropolitan Line trains, Chalfont & Latimer is also served by Chiltern Railway's services that operate between London Marylebone and Aylesbury.

Chalk Farm ● Northern (zone 2)
Opened by the CCE&HR on 22 June 1907, Chalk Farm is situated on the Edgware branch of the Northern. At street level is a fine Leslie Green designed station building that has taken on the wedge shape of the road intersection on which it sits. Those who have fond memories of the 1980s may recognise the station entrance in Adelaide Road, as it formed the cover of Madness's 1980 album 'Absolutely' and also the cover for their hit single 'Baggy Trousers'.

91

A to Z   Chancery Lane *to* Chesham

Chancery Lane ● Central (zone 1)

Opened by the Central London Railway on 30 July 1900, Chancery Lane's eastbound tunnel is directly above the westbound tunnel. This was to avoid the railway having to pass beneath several surface buildings (for which compensation would have had to be paid). This arrangement means that the eastbound tunnel has a steady climb from Holborn, and it is actually possible to see Holborn station from the west end of the eastbound platform and watch your train arrive and depart from Holborn and climb all the way up to Chancery Lane. The original station building was replaced by the current entrance and sub-surface ticket hall beneath the road junction of High Holborn and Gray's Inn Road in 1934, at which time the station was renamed Chancery Lane (Gray's Inn), although the suffix did not last long. The original station building designed by Harry Bell Measures still exists and can be found further along High Holborn carrying the name 'Chancery Station House'.

Charing Cross ● Northern ● Bakerloo (zone 1)

Not only does this station serve the mainline terminus of the same name, but it is also the tube station for the National Gallery, The Strand and Trafalgar Square. The Baker Street & Waterloo Railway first opened a station here with the name 'Trafalgar Square' on 10 March 1906. Next came the Charing Cross, Euston & Hampstead Railway (now part of the Northern Line), which opened a station called 'Charing Cross' nearby in June 1907. This was renamed 'Charing Cross (Strand)' in 1914, and then to just 'Strand' in 1915. Strand station was closed in 1973 to allow construction of

A train of 1972 MkII Stock led by 3536 arrives in the northbound Bakerloo Line platform at Charing Cross on 10 January 2015.

the new Jubilee Line Charing Cross terminus. When this opened in 1979, the three stations all became part of the same complex which took the name 'Charing Cross'. When the Jubilee Line extension opened in 1999, it bypassed the Charing Cross terminus which closed on 20 November 1999. The Jubilee Line platforms are still there, disused by passengers, and hidden behind closed doors. They can still be used to reverse trains (out of service) at times of disruption and are occasionally used to stable engineering trains. The Northern Line platform walls are decorated with murals by David Gentleman depicting the building of the original Charing Cross, and the Bakerloo Line platform walls are decorated with scenes to be viewed at the National Gallery and National Portrait Gallery, which were designed by Richard Dragun and June Fraser.

Chesham ● Metropolitan (zone 9)

One of only two stations in zone 9 (the other being Amersham), Chesham is the furthest point west that passengers can travel to on the London Underground, although empty trains going into the reversing sidings at nearby Amersham travel slightly further west. Since closure of the Central Line's Ongar branch in September 1994, Chesham has also been the most northerly point on the entire Underground. The station at Chesham opened as the northern terminus of the Metropolitan Railway on 8 July 1889. Today it is the only station on the single track branch which turns off from the Metropolitan Line's Amersham line at Chalfont & Latimer. The branch is just under 4 miles long and runs through the rural Chess Valley.

The station still has a signal box and steam age water tower, both disused, but both in fine condition.

A to Z Chigwell *to* Clapham South

Chigwell 🔴 Central (zone 4)
Opened by the Great Eastern Railway on 1 May 1903 as part of its Woodford to Ilford line, Chigwell became a part of the London Underground when the Central Line took over the line between Newbury Park and Woodford, and was first served by tube trains in November 1948. The station still retains a fine example of a Great Eastern Railway station building.

Chiswick Park 🟢 District (zone 4)
Opened by the Metropolitan District Railway on 1 July 1879 as part of that railway's line from Turnham Green to Ealing Broadway, the station was rebuilt to a Charles Holden design in 1931/32 to accommodate the western extension of the Piccadilly Line from Hammersmith. The line through here consists of four tracks (westbound local, westbound fast, eastbound fast and eastbound local). The station only has platforms on the local lines, which are served by District Line trains. The fast lines through the middle are used by Piccadilly Line trains which do not call here. That is the usual method of operation, but it is not unheard of for a Piccadilly Line train to run along the local lines from time to time.

Of particular note here are the heritage signs showing a list of destinations that trains go to from each platform. A small plaque beneath these signs states that the signs have been retained as part of the station's heritage and that Mark Lane is now called Tower Hill. Sadly, the heritage signs have since had Mark Lane crudely covered over with stickers stating Tower Hill.

Chorleywood 🔴 Metropolitan (zone 7)
Opened by the Metropolitan Railway on 8 July 1889 as part of that railway's extension from Rickmansworth to Chesham, Chorleywood has undergone several subtle name changes through the years. It opened as 'Chorley Wood' and became 'Chorley Wood & Chenies' in 1915. In 1934 it reverted to its original name before becoming 'Chorleywood' in 1964. At the south end of the platform 1 there is a disused and boarded up Metropolitan Railway signalbox. Behind platform 1 is the station car park, and this was at one time a goods yard, and there is still a cable arch that takes the trackside cables up and over what used to be the entrance to the goods yard.

Clapham Common ⚫ Northern (zone 2)
The entrance to Clapham Common station is located close to the junction of the A3 and A24 roads at the east end of the common. The western entrance has a very attractive dome and dates from when the station opened in June 1900. Until 1926 when the Morden extension was opened, it was the terminus of the City & South London Railway after that railway had extended to Clapham Common from Stockwell. At platform level, this station still has the original C&SLR style layout with both northbound and southbound tracks in the same tunnel and separated by a narrow island platform.

Clapham North ⚫ Northern (zone 2)
Along with Clapham Common, Clapham North also has a C&SLR style layout with both tracks inside one tunnel and separated by a narrow island platform. At street level, the original station building designed by TP Figgis was remodelled in the 1920s by Charles Holden. The station opened as 'Clapham Road' in 1900 and was renamed 'Clapham North' on 13 September 1926, the day the Morden extension opened.

Clapham South ⚫ Northern (zones 2 and 3)
Located on the southern edge of Clapham Common, this station is the first on the C&SLR's Morden extension, and like all stations on this stretch of line, has a station building designed by Charles

93

A to Z

Two trains of 1995 Stock pass each other at Clapham North on 27 December 2015.

A to Z Cockfosters *to* Covent Garden

Holden that is finished in Portland Stone. Beneath the station is located a deep level air raid shelter, which saw further use after the war to house temporarily some of the first immigrants to come to the UK from Jamaica.

Cockfosters ● Piccadilly (zone 5)

The eastern terminus of the Piccadilly Line, Cockfosters station was opened on 31 July 1933 as the final part of the Piccadilly's eastern extension from Finsbury Park. The station was designed by Charles Holden, and the street level main entrance is a modest single level brick building with a concrete roof with two large roundels mounted on two short towers. There is also a western entrance on the opposite side of the road to the main entrance, which is a simple concrete flat roofed affair with a large roundel mounted on top of it. The western entrance is adjacent to a small bus interchange and a subway beneath the main road links it to the station. The concourse and platform area is far more impressive with a concrete roof which spans the concourse and the three track layout with two island platforms. There are four platform faces, the centre track having a platform face on each side.

Westbound trains actually depart from Cockfosters in an easterly direction, and on the south side of the line between Cockfosters and the next station at Oakwood is Cockfosters Depot. This is one of two main depots on the Piccadilly (the other being at Northfields), and it can be accessed from either the Cockfosters end or the Oakwood end.

Colindale ● Northern (zone 4)

Opened on 18 August 1924, the original station building was destroyed in a German air raid on 25 September 1940. Thirteen people were killed, and they are remembered by a plaque in the station which was unveiled in 2012. The current station building dates from 1962 and replaced a temporary structure that had stood since 1940. To the north of the platforms there is a centre reversing siding to allow trains from the south to turn back, but under normal operating conditions, this is only used to reverse one train per day (Monday to Saturday).

Colliers Wood ● Northern (zone 3)

Situated on the Morden extension, this station has a Charles Holden designed station building which is angular across a street corner. On the opposite side of the High Street to the station entrance is a pub called 'The Charles Holden'.

Covent Garden ● Piccadilly (zone 1)

Although the Great Northern, Piccadilly & Brompton Railway opened their Finsbury Park to Hammersmith line through here on 15 December 1906, this station did not open until 11 April 1907. At street level there is a fine example of a Leslie Green designed station building with distinctive red tiling. This gives access to platform level either by lift or by using the stairs, of which there are 193! The platforms are decorated in a unique tile pattern of white and two shades of yellow. This is typical of 37 Leslie Green stations which had their own unique tiling to help illiterate passengers recognise each station. The original tiling was replaced on a 'like for like' basis during a station refurbishment in 2010. The distance from Covent Garden to the next station at Leicester Square is the shortest distance between two stations on the entire Underground at just 0.16 miles. If you journey between the two stations using a zone 1 cash single fare of £4.90 (as at the start of 2016), then you are paying a fare of over £30 per mile, making it one of the most expensive train journeys in the country! Of course few people would ever be likely to make this journey as it is actually quicker to walk than enter and exit the stations and make the train journey. There are signs posted around both stations advising of the close proximity of the two stations.

A to Z Croxley *to* Dagenham Heathway

The 'Night Tube' liveried train of 1973 Stock arrives in the westbound platform at Covent Garden with a Cockfosters to Northfields service on 30 July 2015.

Croxley 🔴 Metropolitan (zone 7)
This is the only intermediate station on the Watford branch of the Metropolitan. Opened with the line on 2 November 1925 as Croxley Green, the station was renamed just Croxley on 23 May 1949. The station is located in Croxley Green.

Dagenham East 🟢 District (zone 5)
Opened by the London, Tilbury & Southend Railway as 'Dagenham' in 1885, the station was rebuilt by the London, Midland & Scottish Railway in 1932 with an extra pair of tracks to serve the District. There are four tracks through here, the two District tracks, and running parallel are two tracks of the former LT&SR main line, and now a part of Network Rail's Fenchurch Street to Southend route. Today there are only platforms serving the District tracks, the two platforms on the main line having been closed when that line was electrified in 1962. The disused platforms are still in situ. The station was renamed 'Dagenham East' in 1949. There is a bay platform where trains from the west can be turned back, and a handful of trains are timetabled to do so. There is also a siding off of the bay road which was used to store withdrawn D Stock for part of 2015.

Dagenham Heathway 🟢 District (zone 5)
Unlike the next station at Dagenham East, Dagenham Heathway has never had any platforms on the adjacent main line. Opened in 1932 by the LMS as 'Heathway', the station was renamed 'Dagenham Heathway' in 1949. The station building is on the A1240 'Heathway' which crosses over the line at this point, and the island platform is reached by a long sloping ramp from street level down to platform level.

A to Z Debden *to* Ealing Common

Debden 🔴 Central (zone 6)
Opened by the Great Eastern Railway as 'Chigwell Road' in 1865, the name was changed to 'Chigwell Lane' in December 1865, and then changed to 'Debden' on 25 September 1949, the day British Railways steam services were replaced by the tube trains of the Central Line. The rather bland station building dates from 1974, although the original stationmaster's house does still survive alongside it. There is a centre reversing siding on the Epping side of the station which can actually be used to turn back trains from either direction. There are a small number of peak hour services from the west that are timetabled to terminate at Debden and head back west via this siding.

Dollis Hill ⚪ Jubilee (zone 5)
Opened by the Metropolitan Railway in 1909 as 'Dollis Hill', the station was renamed 'Dollis Hill and Gladstone Park' in 1931. It only carried this name for two years before reverting back to 'Dollis Hill'. The station consists of an island platform which serves the Jubilee Line only. The northbound and southbound Metropolitan tracks pass by on the outside of the Jubilee tracks. The Network Rail lines in and out of Marylebone also run parallel to the Underground tracks on the northbound side of the station.

Ealing Broadway 🔴 Central 🟢 District (zone 3)
The first Underground line to reach Ealing Broadway was the Metropolitan District Railway on 1 July 1879. The Central Line reached here much later when the GWR's Ealing & Shepherd's Bush Railway reached here on 3 August 1920. Today the station is still served by the Central and the District, and they both interchange with the Network Rail station on the parallel Great Western main line in and out of Paddington. Network Rail services, which pass through or call here include First Great Western, Heathrow Connect and Heathrow Express along with a fair amount of freight traffic. The Network Rail tracks pass through platforms 1 to 4 which are all through lines. The Central Line terminates in platforms 5 and 6 and the District Line terminates in platforms 7, 8 and 9. Platform 7 is out in the open, but the west end of platforms 8 and 9 are covered by the original train shed. Look out for some 1908 style replica roundels on the District Line platforms. Until 2010, there was a physical connection between the District and Central lines here, but this was removed in 2010. This connection used to branch off of one of two sidings (numbered 24 and 25) at the east end of the District Line platforms. After the removal of the connection between the two lines, the two sidings survived, but saw very little use, and were eventually removed during 2015.

Ealing Common 🔵 Piccadilly 🟢 District (zone 3)
Served by both the Piccadilly and District lines, Ealing Common was opened by the Metropolitan District Railway with their line to Ealing Broadway on 1 July 1879. The station was rebuilt in 1930/31

Left: A train of 1992 Stock with 91171 on the rear departs from Ealing Broadway. Note the District Line D Stock train to the left. Right: Ealing Common's heptagonal station building.

97

A to Z Earl's Court *to* East Acton

and features a heptagonal station building made from Portland Stone. At the east end of the station is the western entrance / exit to and from Ealing Common depot, and some District Line trains start and finish their journeys here at the start and end of traffic. To the west of the station, the line crosses over the Great Western main line and the Central Line, and then the District's branch to Ealing Broadway diverges to the left leaving the Piccadilly to carry on towards South Harrow, Rayners Lane and Uxbridge.

Earl's Court ● Piccadilly ● District (zones 1 and 2)

The Metropolitan District Railway opened their branch from South Kensington to West Brompton through here on 12 April 1869, but there was no station here until 30 October 1871.

This first station was located in the cutting to the east of the current station, and was closed following a fire in 1875. Rather than rebuild the station in the same location, which was deemed to be too cramped, the replacement station was constructed on the opposite side of the Earl's Court Road and opened on 1 February 1878. Earl's Court is the hub of the District Line, with all branches converging here. The District Line part of the station has four platforms, and is situated in a cutting under a fine overall glass and steel roof. Platforms 3 and 4 are westbound and trains can go towards either Wimbledon or Hammersmith/Olympia from either platform. Trains arriving from the Gloucester Road direction can reach both platforms 3 and 4, but trains coming from the High Street Kensington direction can only access platform 4. In the eastbound direction, trains use platforms 1 and 2. Trains from the Hammersmith / Olympia route can access both platforms, but trains from the Wimbledon branch can only enter platform 2. Upon departure, eastbound trains can travel towards either Gloucester Road or High Street Kensington from either platform.

Of note on the District Line platforms are the old style train describers (pictured right) with illuminated arrows to point to the destination of the next train, which still perform this function today. There are several modern dot matrix indicators giving a little bit more detail positioned along each platform, but these, while being very visible, are quite discreet and do not detract from the overall heritage feel of the station.

The Piccadilly Line also calls at Earl's Court, and trains use platforms 5 (eastbound) and 6 (westbound), both of which are directly beneath the District Line platforms, albeit in tube tunnel. The Piccadilly platforms opened here when the Great Northern, Piccadilly & Brompton Railway opened its tube line from Finsbury Park to Hammersmith on 15 December 1906.

East Acton ● Central (zone 2)

This station is notable for having a replica Great Western Railway waiting shelter on each platform (dating from 1976), which reflects the fact that the section of line from Wood Lane to Ealing Broadway was built by the Great Western Railway, and initially the Central London Railway only had running powers over it. The CLR shared tracks with GWR freight traffic until an extra pair of tracks was added in 1938 onto which the freight traffic was diverted. These tracks were closed and lifted in 1964, and the space that they used to occupy behind the eastbound platform is now very overgrown.

A to Z Eastcote *to* East Ham

Eastcote ● Metropolitan ● Piccadilly (zone 5)

Although the Metropolitan Railway opened its line through here between Harrow-on-the-Hill and Uxbridge on 4 July 1904, there was initially only one intermediate stop (at Ruislip). Eastcote station opened on 26 May 1906 and was originally called 'Eastcote Halt'. The main station building which fronts on to Field End Road, dates from a rebuild in 1939 and was designed by Charles Holden.

East Finchley ● Northern (zone 3)

Originally opened by the Great Northern Railway as East End, Finchley on 22 August 1867, this station was on the GNR's line between Finsbury Park and Edgware (via Highgate). In 1886, the station was renamed to 'East Finchley', and in 1923, following the '1921 Railways Act', became a part of the London, North Eastern Railway (LNER). All of this happened prior to the Underground reaching here, which it did from 3 July 1939, when the station became the temporary terminus of the Northern Line's extension from Highgate. Northern Line trains continued beyond East Finchley, to High Barnet, from 14 April 1940.

There are four platforms at East Finchley. The two centre platforms (2 and 3) give access to and from Highgate Sidings and are only used by trains that stable at Highgate Sidings as they enter or leave service. All other trains use platform 4 (southbound), and platform 1 (northbound). To the north of the station, there is a disused and boarded up former Great Northern Railway signal box which is visible from the car park and the platform ends. Standing above platform 4, is 'The Archer', a statue of a kneeling archer firing his arrow towards Central London which was designed by Eric Aumonier (pictured right).

East Ham ● District ● Hammersmith & City (zones 3 and 4)

Originally opened by the London, Tilbury & Southend Railway, the current buildings and platforms served by the District were a later addition and date back to 1905 when the District tracks were electrified. East Ham served as the eastern terminus of the District from 1905 until 1908 when the electrified tracks were extended through to Barking. Parallel to the Underground tracks here are the Network Rail lines in and out of Fenchurch Street, and up until 1962, trains on this line used to call at East Ham, and the

99

A to Z East Putney *to* Edgware Road

remains of the main line platforms can still be seen from passing trains. There is also an abandoned bay platform adjacent to the eastbound Underground platform that was served by trains to and from the Gospel Oak to Barking line via an abandoned curve that used to be known as the East Ham Loop, and which joined the Gospel Oak to Barking line at East Ham Loop North Junction. This line closed in 1958.

There are several items at East Ham that are worth looking out for. The platform canopies are held up by brackets that have the letters LTSR cast into them, a painted sign advertises tea at 2d (two old pence) per cup, and to the west of the platforms, adjacent to the westbound track is a water tower that was installed to top up the water tanks of steam locomotives. Having not filled a steam locomotive's tank for many, many years, this is a truly remarkable survivor. It is visible from the west end of the platforms at East Ham.

East Putney ● District (zones 2 and 3)

Located about half a mile to the south of the Fulham Rail Bridge, East Putney is situated on the Wimbledon branch of the District. Immediately to the south of the station is East Putney Junction where a chord between the District and Network Rail's Point Pleasant Junction on the Clapham Junction to Barnes line diverges. This is used by empty stock trains travelling to and from Wimbledon depot, and reflects the fact that this section of line was built by the London & South Western Railway (LSWR) and the District only had running powers over it. The line passed over to the Southern Railway and then British Railways until it was sold to London Underground in 1994 with main line trains keeping their access to the route for empty stock movements only. The Southern Railway ceased operating passenger trains over the route in 1941. The station has three platforms, with platforms 1 and 2 serving the District, and the disused platform 3 (the opposite face of platform 2) adjacent to the East Putney Junction to Point Pleasant Junction track. There are also the abandoned remains of the fourth platform in the undergrowth adjacent to the track from Point Pleasant Junction to East Putney Junction.

Edgware ● Northern (zone 5)

The terminus of the Charing Cross, Euston & Hampstead Railway's extension from Golders Green, Edgware opened to traffic on 18 August 1924. The station consists of three platforms, with platform 1 being out in the open, and platforms 2 and 3 situated beneath a train shed. A fan of sidings alongside the station provides stabling for trains outside of traffic hours. There are also three engineers' sidings that serve Edgware Track Depot.

Edgware's station building was designed by Stanley Heaps and fronts onto the A5100 Station Road. It is possible to interchange here between the Underground and local bus services via Edgware bus station which is located alongside the station.

Edgware Road ● Bakerloo (zone 1)

Opened on 15 June 1907 as a terminus, Edgware Road became a through station from 1 December 1913 when the Baker Street & Waterloo Railway extended to Paddington. At street level, the station still retains its original red tiled building designed by Leslie Green. The Underground does of course have two stations at Edgware Road, this one serving the Bakerloo Line, and just a short walk away, the sub-surface station serving the Hammersmith & City, Circle and District lines. The Underground map does not show an interchange between the two lines and there is no direct link between the two.

Edgware Road ● District ● Hammersmith & City ● Circle (zone 1)

Located in a cutting alongside the A40 Marylebone Road, close to its junction with the A5 Edgware

A to Z Elephant & Castle *to* Embankment

Road, this station acts as both a through station and a terminus. Under normal operating conditions, platform 1 is a through platform for Circle and Hammersmith & City trains coming from the Hammersmith branch and travelling on the outer rail of the inner circle towards King's Cross St Pancras. Platform 2 is used to terminate Circle Line trains which have travelled around the inner circle on the outer rail and are about to return via the inner rail. Platform 3 is used to terminate District Line trains on the Wimbledon to Edgware Road route, and platform 4 is used by Hammersmith & City and Circle line trains on the inner rail heading for Hammersmith. Opposite platform 4 is number 26 siding which is used to stable one train outside of traffic hours.

Originally opened as part of the Metropolitan Railway's first line in 1863, Edgware Road was home of the MR's engine sheds, but these were moved to Neasden due to a lack of space. The station today bears little resemblance to the station that first opened to the public on 10 January 1863.

Elephant & Castle ● Northern ● Bakerloo (zones 1 and 2)

There is interchange between the Northern and Bakerloo lines here, and it is also possible, via a short walk, to interchange with trains calling at the nearby Network Rail station.

The Northern Line platforms (numbered 1 and 2) were the first to be built, and they were opened by the City & South London Railway as part of the world's first deep level tube railway which ran between King William Street and Stockwell. The Bakerloo platforms (numbered 3 and 4) were opened by the Baker Street & Waterloo Railway on 5 August 1906, and although the two sets of platforms belonged to separate companies, they were connected by foot tunnels below ground from 1906. Look out for the original City & South London Railway tiles (pictured below), which are located in the emergency stairs from the Northern Line platforms to street level.

At street level, there are two station buildings separated by a large roundabout. The most northerly of the two buildings is the original Leslie Green designed station building built for the opening of the BS&WR in 1906.

The Bakerloo Line platforms form the southern terminus of the Bakerloo. The line continues for a short distance to the south of the platforms where up to two trains can be stabled in the northbound and southbound sidings. At the north end of the station is a scissors crossover allowing trains to arrive and depart from either platform.

Elm Park ● District (zone 6)

This station is the newest station on the section of the District Line between Barking and Upminster, and was opened by the LMS in 1935. Elm Park has only ever had platforms serving the District tracks and has never had platforms serving the adjacent Network Rail tracks. The station consists of an island platform, reached by a sloping walkway from the station building, located on The Broadway which crosses over the railway here.

Embankment ● District ● Circle ● Northern ● Bakerloo (zone 1)

A station with a rather complex history, this station is situated on the north bank of the River Thames, beneath the platform ends of Charing Cross main line station. The station first opened as Charing Cross on 30 May 1870 when the Metropolitan District Railway extended its line from Westminster to Blackfriars. This is the sub-surface part of the station, which is today served by trains on the Circle and District lines. Next to open was the Bakerloo Line station which was opened by the

A to Z Epping

Baker Street & Waterloo Railway as Embankment on 10 March 1906. Although the sub-surface station was called Charing Cross, and the BS&WR station was called Embankment, there was an interchange provided between the two railways. The Northern Line station was opened by the Charing Cross, Euston & Hampstead Railway on 6 April 1914. Although this was built as a terminus of the CCE&HR, the station consisted of a single through platform located on a balloon shaped loop. The new CCE&HR station was opened as Charing Cross (Embankment) and the BS&WR station also changed its name to match, although the sub-surface station retained the name Charing Cross. In 1915, the Embankment in brackets was dropped so that the deep level station and the sub-surface station all had the same name.

In preparation for a further extension of the CCE&HR south of here (to join up with the City & South London Railway at Kennington), the original CCE&HR platform became the northbound platform and a new southbound platform was constructed in 1925. The southbound platform is on a straight alignment, but the northbound platform, being on what used to be part of the balloon shaped loop, is curved.

In 1974, the whole station was renamed yet again to Charing Cross (Embankment), and then renamed to just Embankment in 1976. This latter name change was to facilitate the renaming of the Bakerloo's Trafalgar Square station, and the Northern's Strand station to Charing Cross, when they were merged together, to form a complex with the then under construction terminus of the new Jubilee Line.

To the south of this station, the Bakerloo passes beneath the River Thames, and at some points the tunnels are just a few feet below the bottom of the river bed. With the fear that German bombing could penetrate the tunnels, floodgates were installed here, and at Waterloo in 1939. The floodgates are still in situ. On the curved northbound Northern Line platform, the old 'Mind the Gap' announcement recorded by Oswald Laurence can still be heard when trains arrive. These announcements could at one time be heard at several stations across the Underground, but have been phased out. The recording at Embankment was restored to use at the request of Mr Laurence's widow so that she could hear his voice whenever she passes through the station.

The two Northern Line platforms at Embankment, with the straight southbound platform on the left, and the curved northbound platform on the right.

Epping ● Central (zone 6)

Epping station opened on 24 April 1865 when the Great Eastern Railway opened an extension of its line from Loughton to Ongar. The line was transferred to the Underground's Central Line on 25 September 1949, although electrification did not go beyond Epping to Ongar until 1957. Until then, a hired in British Railways steam loco and coaching stock was used between Epping & Ongar, with passengers travelling to Ongar from locations west of Epping having to change trains at Epping (and vice versa). Closure of the Ongar branch came on 30 September 1994, and from that date, Epping became the eastern terminus of the Central Line. Looking towards Ongar from the platforms at Epping, it will be noted that the tracks continue beyond the red stop lights, with the track through platform 2 continuing into the now disused east siding, and the track through platform 1 continuing through to Ongar. The Ongar branch is now a privately owned railway operated by preserved diesel and steam traction (see eorrailway.co.uk). Trains on the Epping & Ongar Railway do not run into Epping station, but when the railway is operating, visitors can reach the EOR from Epping station by using the vintage bus service which operates between Epping station and North Weald station. After closure in 1994, no trains ran through to the Ongar branch, although the track was left in place. During the early hours of 25 September 2014, the stop lights at the end of platform 1 were lowered, and a special train was allowed to work through hauled by two Schöma diesel locomotives which conveyed the preserved 3-car Cravens 1960 Stock train (with 1938 Stock trailer) to the railway to take part in an event to celebrate 20 years since the closure of the line by London Underground. Since then, the connection between the two railways has seen further limited use by engineering trains.

At the west end of the station is Epping signal cabin. This is no longer used by the Underground and is now in the hands of Cravens Heritage Trains who are restoring the building into a museum. Standing on a plinth between the signal cabin and the running lines is loco L11 which is being restored as a static exhibit. This is an electric shunting locomotive which was made from two redundant Standard Stock driving motors to make one vehicle with a cab at each end. In this guise, it saw use as a shunter at Acton Works.

Epping station is the only station served by tube trains to be outside of the M25 London Orbital motorway. The railway passes beneath the M25 about ¾ mile west of Epping.

Euston ● Northern ● Victoria (zone 1)

Euston has six platforms on the Underground, platforms 1 and 2 serve the Northern Line's Charing Cross branch, platforms 3 and 6 serve the Northern Line's Bank branch and platforms 4 and 5 serve the Victoria Line.

The first tube line to serve Euston was the City & South London Railway which reached here on 12 May 1907 when an extension from Angel to Euston was opened. This station was a typical C&SLR station with two tracks inside one tunnel with an island platform between them. This station was a terminus until the line was extended to join up with the CCE&HR at Camden Town, this extension opening on 20 April 1924. The island platform remained in place until the 1960s when the station was rebuilt to accommodate the new Victoria Line. The southbound line still uses the original station tunnel (platform 6), but the northbound line was diverted into newly built tunnel on the opposite side of the new Victoria Line platforms, resulting in platform 6 being very wide, where the positions of the former northbound track have been filled in. The original northbound track is still in place to the south side of the station, and this forms the Euston loop which can be used by engineering trains travelling between the southbound Northern and the Piccadilly Line (via the King's Cross loop).

The second tube line to serve Euston was the CCE&HR which opened its line between Charing Cross and Golders Green and Highgate on 22 June 1907. Although the station complex is now reached via entrances in Euston mainline station, the original Leslie Green designed CCE&HR station building is still in situ on the corner of Melton Street and Drummond Street (pictured right).

A to Z Euston Square *to* Farringdon

The Victoria Line opened through Euston on 1 December 1968. Victoria Line trains run on the right through Euston in order to give cross platform interchange between the southbound Victoria and southbound Northern (Bank branch), and between the northbound Victoria and northbound Northern (Bank branch). The Victoria Line tunnels revert to left hand running to the north of King's Cross St Pancras and to the south of Warren Street. Although the Northern (Bank branch) and the Victoria are both north to south railways, both lines actually pass through Euston in opposite directions on an east to west axis.

Euston Square ● Metropolitan ● Hammersmith & City ● Circle (zone 1)

Opened as part of the world's first underground railway, the station opened as Gower Street on 10 January 1863. The name was changed to Euston Square in November 1909. There are many original features still in place at this station, but they are hidden beneath modern looking tiling which gives the station a rather Spartan appearance at platform level. At street level, there are no station buildings, just a subway entrance on the north side of Euston Road, and an entrance in the bottom of the Wellcome Trust building on Gower Street. There is no direct link between Euston Square and Euston station, but it is only a short walk between the two.

Fairlop ● Central (zone 4)

This station was opened by the Great Eastern Railway in May 1903 as part of that railway's Woodford to Ilford route. Steam trains ceased running through here in November 1947, with Central Line trains operating in passenger service from 31 May 1948, although Central Line trains had been running empty through here to reach Hainault depot from December 1947. The station still retains many original features, including the letters GER cast into the platform canopy support brackets.

It could have all been so different though, as a proposal prior to the Second World War was to have seen Fairlop become the location of a passenger airport for London. Instead, the proposed site became an RAF fighter station during the war. By the time hostilities had ceased, the site was no longer considered to be suitable for a role as a major airport and a site at Heathrow was chosen instead. The RAF station closed in 1946 and the site is now occupied by the Fairlop Waters country park and golf course located immediately to the east of the station.

Farringdon ● Metropolitan ● Hammersmith & City ● Circle (zone 1)

The first station to open here was called Farringdon Street and it was the eastern terminus of the Metropolitan Railway's line from Paddington Bishop's Road. This was the world's first underground railway which opened to the public on 10 January 1863. The original station was in a slightly different position to the current station, the change in location taking place when the MR opened their extension to Aldersgate Street in December 1865.

The station was renamed Farringdon & High Holborn in 1926, a name which can still be seen adorning the station building in Cowcross Street, along with a sign for 'Parcels Office' on the side of the building. The current name of Farringdon was adopted from April 1936.

As well as serving the Metropolitan, Hammersmith & City and Circle lines, Farringdon is also served by Thameslink on what used to be known as the 'City Widened Lines', and there is interchange between the Underground and Thameslink. The 'City Widened Lines' got their name when the Metropolitan Railway increased the width of the cutting to accommodate two extra tracks. These tracks were used by other railways as well as the Metropolitan, and linked both the Great Northern Railway and the Midland Railway with the London, Chatham & Dover Railway. Today they are used by Thameslink services and the link with the former GNR no longer exists. To the west of Farringdon, the Thameslink line, which has been on the north side of the Underground lines from King's Cross, dives down beneath the Underground lines to emerge on the south side on the approach to Farringdon station. The point where they pass beneath the Underground lines has been known as

A to Z Finchley Central *to* Finchley Road

the 'Ray Street Gridiron', which when built was the world's first triple deck cast iron bridge, although the structure today is mostly made of concrete. Beneath both railways here is the River Fleet, which is an underground sewer which runs from Hampstead Heath to the River Thames at Blackfriars Bridge.

The 'Widened Lines' used to run to Moorgate, and at the west end of the station was a junction where the line towards Blackfriars split away from the Moorgate line. Today this junction is no more with only the line towards Blackfriars remaining. This was to allow the Thameslink platforms to be extended over the site of the former junction to accommodate longer trains. The Farringdon to Moorgate section closed in March 2009. Also to the west of the station are Farringdon Sidings. These were formerly used to stable C Stock trains, but not being long enough to stable the longer S Stock trains that replaced the C Stock, they fell out of use and at the time of compiling this book, were still in situ, but were expected to be removed.

Eventually, both the Underground and Thameslink lines will be able to interchange at Farringdon with the currently under construction Crossrail route.

With The Shard and St Paul's Cathedral as a backdrop, this view looking down on Farringdon station shows a Thameslink class 319 on the 'widened lines', while two trains of S Stock pass each other on the Underground's side of the station.

Finchley Central ● Northern (zone 4)

This station boasts a fine set of former Great Northern Railway style station buildings, having been opened by the Edgware, Highgate & London Railway (later to become part of the GNR) on 22 August 1867 as part of that railway's line to Edgware. Today the station is the junction for the Mill Hill East branch (all that remains of the former line to Edgware), and the High Barnet branch (which was opened by the GNR on 1 April 1872). The station was served by Underground trains from 14 April 1940.

There are three platforms, with platform 1 usually only used by trains serving the Mill Hill East branch. There are two reversing sidings, one at each end of the station.

Finchley Road ● Metropolitan ● Jubilee (zone 2)

A four platform station served by both the Jubilee and Metropolitan lines, with the two Jubilee platforms (2 and 3) sitting between the two Metropolitan platforms (1 and 4). To the south of the station, the Jubilee Line dives down in to tube tunnel, while the Metropolitan carries on to Baker Street in sub surface tunnel (with some short open air stretches). To the north, the tracks of the

A to Z Finsbury Park *to* Gloucester Road

Jubilee Line are between the northbound and southbound Metropolitan tracks until just north of Wembley Park. Alongside Finchley Road station, the two track Network Rail line in and out of Marylebone come alongside the formation to make a six track wide formation.

At one time there was a pair of crossovers at Finchley Road allowing trains to cross from the Jubilee to the Metropolitan in the southbound direction, and from the Metropolitan to the Jubilee in the northbound direction. The crossovers have been removed, but there is still a gantry above the southbound Jubilee track that used to carry three glass tubes that if broken by a full size train of Surface Stock, would put signals to danger and raise the train stops to prevent a full size train from entering the tube tunnels (tube trains were low enough to pass beneath the tubes). The glass tubes are no longer in place, but their mounting points on the underside of the gantry can still be clearly seen.

Finsbury Park ● Piccadilly ● Victoria (zone 2)

There is a physical link here between the Piccadilly and Victoria lines, which is used by engineering trains to access the Victoria Line. There is interchange here between the two lines, and also with the Network Rail station. The Piccadilly was altered here in the 1960s to accommodate the Victoria Line. The former Great Northern & City Railway tunnels, which were built to accommodate full height trains (as opposed to tube sized trains), were taken over by the westbound Piccadilly and the southbound Victoria. The old Piccadilly westbound platform became the northbound Victoria and the eastbound Piccadilly remained as the eastbound Piccadilly. Evidence of the former Great Northern & City Railway is apparent in the size of the overall bore of the westbound Piccadilly and southbound Victoria, which are both much larger than the trains that use them. Mosaics of hot air balloons line the walls of the Piccadilly Line platforms to mark the fact that Finsbury Park was the location of one of the first hot air balloon flights.

Fulham Broadway ● District (zone 2)

Situated on the District Line's Wimbledon branch, Fulham Broadway is the station to use for Chelsea's Stamford Bridge football ground. The station opened as Walham Green in March 1880. In order to cope better with match day crowds, the station was rebuilt in 1905 and was renamed to Fulham Broadway in March 1952. The Fulham Broadway shopping complex has been built over part of the station, giving the Earl's Court end of the station a very bland and modern appearance, but the Wimbledon end of the station is in a time warp and still retains many of the features from the 1905 rebuild, such as the overall roof and side walls.

Gants Hill ● Central (zone 4)

Located on the section of tube tunnel between Leytonstone and Newbury Park that was built, but not fitted out at the start of the war, and was used as an underground bomb proof aircraft components factory, Gants Hill was eventually opened to traffic on 14 December 1947. The circulating area between the platforms has been finished to a design by Charles Holden that is based on the style of a Moscow Metro station.

Gloucester Road ● Circle ● District ● Piccadilly (zone 1)

This sub-surface station was opened by the Metropolitan Railway on 1 October 1868, as a part of that railway's extension from Praed Street Junction to South Kensington. The station was also served by Metropolitan District Railway trains when that railway opened an extension westwards from South Kensington to West Brompton on 12 April 1869. On 15 December 1906, the Great Northern, Piccadilly & Brompton Railway opened its tube line from Finsbury Park to Hammersmith which included a station at Gloucester Road. The two railways had separate entrances at street level, and

A to Z Golders Green *to* Great Portland Street

this can still be evidenced today, although the former GNP&BR station is today used as retail outlets, with public access to and from both the sub-surface and tube platforms being through the former Metropolitan & District Railway station building. Today the station is still served by the Piccadilly at tube level, and by the District and Circle lines at sub-surface level. The west end of the station is where the Circle and District diverge from each other, with the District heading to and from Earl's Court and the Circle heading to and from High Street Kensington. The sub-surface platforms were rafted over and apartments and a shopping mall built over the top in the 1990s, but some old features remain at platform level, including the old retaining walls and old style train describers on platform 1.

Golders Green ● Northern (zone 3)

Opened as the northern terminus of the Charing Cross, Euston & Hampstead Railway on 22 June 1907, Golders Green became a through station when the line was extended towards Edgware, initially to Hendon on 19 November 1923. Alongside the station is Golders Green depot, one of two main depots on the Northern Line. To the south of the station, the Northern enters tube tunnel, and there are three tunnel mouths, the most easterly of which is the Golders Green depot headshunt, which is only long enough to accommodate about one car.

Goldhawk Road ● Hammersmith & City ● Circle (zone 2)

The first stop on the Hammersmith branch after departing from Hammersmith, Goldhawk Road opened in April 1914 and replaced the original Shepherd's Bush station which was situated roughly half way between Goldhawk Road and the current Shepherd's Bush Market station (which opened on the same day as Goldhawk Road). This is the closest station to Queen's Park Rangers' Loftus Road football ground.

Goodge Street ● Northern (zone 1)

Opened by the Charing Cross, Euston & Hampstead Railway as Tottenham Court Road on 22 June 1907, the station was renamed Goodge Street on 9 March 1908, the same day that the current Tottenham Court Road had its name changed from Oxford Street. Goodge Street retains its Leslie Green station building at street level.

Grange Hill ● Central (zone 4)

Situated on the Hainault loop at the Woodford end of Hainault Depot, some trains enter or leave service here as they come off or go onto Hainault Depot at the start and end of traffic. Grange Hill station was opened by the Great Eastern Railway on 1 May 1903. It was first served by Central Line trains from 21 November 1948. At platform level, the station retains many GER features, but the station building is a more modern affair dating from 1949, the original GER station building having been flattened by a German V1 flying bomb during the war.

Great Portland Street ● Metropolitan ● Hammersmith & City ● Circle (zone 1)

Opened as part of the world's first Underground railway on 10 January 1863, this station was originally called Portland Road, being renamed Great Portland Street on 1 March 1917. It was also given the name Great Portland Street & Regent's Park in 1923, but reverted to Great Portland Street in 1933. The station retains many 1863 features at platform level, however, the station building is a much later addition which dates from 1930.

A to Z Greenford *to* **Hainault**

Great Portland Street westbound (inner rail) platform

Greenford 🔴 Central (zone 4)
This station is situated close to the Network Rail Junction where the line from Old Oak Common is joined on a triangular junction by a line from West Ealing. This latter line still has a regular passenger service and trains from Paddington terminate in a bay platform between the two Central Line platforms. Until 2014, Greenford was the home of the last wooden escalator on the Underground, but this has now been replaced by an inclined lift.

Green Park 🔵 Piccadilly 🔵 Victoria ⚪ Jubilee (zone 1)
Change here for Buckingham Palace! Opened as Dover Street (St James's) by the Great Northern, Piccadilly & Brompton Railway on 15 December 1906, the station was renamed Green Park on 18 September 1933. Until 1969, the station was served only by the Piccadilly Line, but in 1969, the Victoria Line opened through here from 7 March and interchange was possible between the two lines. A third line was added from 1 May 1979 when the Jubilee Line opened to Charing Cross. Now the last station on the original Jubilee Line before the Jubilee Line Extension (JLE) is reached, this station is today a very important interchange between the Piccadilly, Victoria and Jubilee lines.

Gunnersbury 🟢 District (zone 3)
Opened by the London & South Western Railway on 1 June 1877, today Gunnersbury is served by both the District Line and London Overground services, and is where, just to the north of the station, the District and London Overground services part company at Gunnersbury Junction.

Hainault 🔴 Central (zone 4)
This three platform station still retains many Great Eastern Railway features on platform 1. The bulk of trains from the west terminate here, with a roughly 20 minute interval service continuing on via Chigwell to Woodford. To the north of the platforms is the large Hainault Depot, one of two main depots serving the Central Line.

A to Z Hammersmith *to* Harlesden

Hammersmith ● Hammersmith & City ● Circle (zone 2)
This is a three platform terminus station located on the opposite side of the Hammersmith Broadway to the Hammersmith station that serves the District and Piccadilly lines. It is a very short walk between the two stations, although there is no physical connection between the two. To accommodate the new S Stock trains which are longer than the C Stock trains that they replaced, the buffer stops were moved further towards the Broadway. When the Hammersmith branch opened in 1864, the original terminus was sited slightly further to the north, with the station being relocated to the present site in 1868. The current station dates from a rebuild by the GWR in 1907, and to this day, bench seats with the letters GWR cast into them can still be found on the platforms. At the north end of the station is a footbridge which is very lightly used as passengers enter the station at the buffer stop end and go straight to the next departing train. This footbridge used to extend westwards to link the station with the Grove Road platforms on the L&SWR's Addison Road to Richmond line. Beyond the north end of the station is Hammersmith Depot, which has now been reduced to stabling point status.

Hammersmith ● District ● Piccadilly (zone 2)
A modern four platform station, where cross platform interchange between the District and the Piccadilly lines is possible. Travelling west from here, the Piccadilly runs non-stop to Acton Town, with the District calling at all stations. Interchange with the Circle and Hammersmith & City lines is also possible via a short walk. It is also easy to interchange with local bus services at the adjacent Hammersmith bus station. The station itself is located within the Hammersmith Broadway shopping complex, a development which wiped out the original station buildings. Look out for a section of the original building that has been incorporated into one of the walls close to the station entrance exit.

Hampstead ● Northern (zones 2 and 3)
The deepest station on the entire London Underground at 58.5 metres below the surface. If you fancy some exercise, then take the stairs instead of the lift, there are only 320 of them! The depth of this station is more to do with the ground going up than the railway going down, as by the next station at Golders Green, the line emerges into daylight. Between Hampstead and Golders Green, there is another station that never opened called North End (often referred to as Bull & Bush). Had this opened, then it would have taken the title for deepest station away from Hampstead as it is 67 metres below the ground. Hampstead station was to have been called Heath Street, and tiles on the platform walls that have been restored in recent years show this proposed name. On the surface, this station boasts a fine example of a Leslie Green station building.

Hanger Lane ● Central (zone 3)
Located beneath the Hanger Lane gyratory where the A40 Western Avenue meets the A406 North Circular Road, the station building is in the centre of the gyratory and is reached by several passenger subways.

Harlesden ● Bakerloo (zone 3)
Located on the Watford DC Line to the north of Willesden Junction, Harlesden station was opened by the London & North Western Railway on 15 June 1912, but was not served Bakerloo trains until 16 April 1917. The station retains many LNWR features.

A to Z Harrow & Wealdstone *to* Hatton Cross

Harrow & Wealdstone Bakerloo (zone 5)

The northern terminus of the Bakerloo Line. London Overground services continue beyond here to Watford Junction, while Bakerloo Line trains go into a centre reversing siding to the north of the station where the driver changes ends ready to form the next southbound working. Interchange is available here with the Overground, and also with various local electric services that call at the adjacent Network Rail platforms. The Bakerloo and Overground serve platforms 1 and 2, with Network Rail services using platforms 3 to 6.

Harrow & Wealdstone will forever be remembered for the terrible crash that happened here on the morning of 8 October 1952 when a Perth to Euston express crashed into the rear of a local train that was stationary in the station. The wreckage was then run into by a Euston to Manchester and Liverpool express. In total, 112 people lost their lives that day and more than 300 people were seriously injured. A memorial plaque is located on the station building.

Harrow-on-the-Hill Metropolitan (zone 5)

Harrow-on-the-Hill has six platforms and is served by Chiltern Railways services as well as Metropolitan Line trains, and interchange is possible between the two here. Platform 1 is served by northbound Chiltern Railways services and can also be served by northbound Metropolitan Line trains that are going to run fast north of Harrow-on-the-Hill. Platform 2 is served by southbound Chiltern Railways services, and can also be served by Metropolitan Line trains, but only by trains from the north that are terminating at Harrow-on-the-Hill as the conductor rails end at the south end of the platform. Platforms 3 and 4 are usually used by northbound Metropolitan trains with southbound Metropolitan trains serving platforms 5 and 6. There is a reversing siding located between platforms 4 and 5 at the north end of the station. The platforms still retain their light box train describers (as illustrated).

North of the station is the junction where the Uxbridge branch diverges from the main route to Watford, Chesham, Amersham and Aylesbury.

Harrow-on-the-Hill was opened by the Metropolitan Railway as just Harrow on 2 August 1880, with the current name being applied from 1 June 1894.

Hatton Cross Piccadilly (zones 5 and 6)

This was the first station on the Heathrow extension to open and formed the terminus of the line from 19 July 1975 until the opening of Heathrow Central on 16 December 1977. Further development took place with the opening of Heathrow Terminal 4 on 12 April 1986, the junction for the Terminal 4 loop being just west of Hatton Cross. Look out for the former 'Speedbird' emblem of Imperial Airways, British Overseas Airways Corporation (BOAC) and British Airways in the tiling.

A to Z Heathrow *to* High Street Kensington

Heathrow Terminals 2 & 3 ● Piccadilly (zone 6)
That's not an error in this station's title, as the 2016 Underground map lists this station as Heathrow Terminals 2 & 3 as opposed to its former name of Heathrow Terminals 1,2,3. This is no doubt due to the fact that Terminal 1 closed in June 2015 and is to be demolished to make way for a larger Terminal 2.

This station was opened by HM Queen Elizabeth II on 16 December 1977 as Heathrow Central. It was renamed to Heathrow Central Terminals 1,2,3 in September 1983, and then to just Heathrow Terminals 1,2,3 on 12 April 1986, the day that Heathrow Terminal 4 was opened.

Heathrow Terminal 4 ● Piccadilly (zone 6)
Opened on 12 April 1986, Terminal 4 is located on a single track clockwise loop which branches off the main line to the west of Hatton Cross. Trains arriving here immediately form a train back towards Central London via Terminals 2 & 3.

Heathrow Terminal 5 ● PIccadIlly (zone 6)
Opened on 27 March 2008, the Terminal 5 branch is the newest section of the Underground. It has two platforms, platform 5 is set down only, and platform 6 is pick up only. Trains reverse in a pair of reversing sidings to the west of the station.

Hendon Central ● Northern (zones 3 and 4)
This was the temporary terminus of the Northern's Edgware branch from 19 November 1923 until 18 August 1924. To the north of the platforms, the line goes back into tube tunnel. This is known as Burroughs Tunnel and takes the Northern Line beneath the Midland Main Line and the M1 motorway.

High Barnet ● Northern (zone 5)
Terminus of the Northern Line, High Barnet was opened by the Great Northern Railway on 1 April 1872. It became a part of the Underground from the 14 April 1940. The station buildings are of GNR origin, as is the disused signal box at the south end of platform 1.

High Street Kensington ● Circle ● District (zone 1)
First opened by the Metropolitan Railway on 1 October 1868, High Street Kensington today consists of four platforms. Platforms 1 and 2 are through platforms and are served by Circle Line trains and District Line trains operating between Edgware Road and Wimbledon. Platforms 3 and 4 are bay platforms served by terminating District Line services. To the south of the station is the junction where District Line trains go to and from Earl's Court and Circle Line trains go to and from Gloucester Road.

111

A to Z **Highbury** *to* **Holborn**

Highbury & Islington 🔵 Victoria (zone 2)
The Victoria Line interchanges here with the former Great Northern & City Line (now served by Great Northern class 313 EMUs) and London Overground services on the East London and North London lines. The original GN&CR station building still survives (disused) on the opposite side of the road to the current station entrance. The Victoria Line seat recesses show a castle on a hill (pictured right). The term 'bury' was an old English word meaning castle or manor. In 1271 a manor was built on a hill nearby (destroyed in 1381), giving the name of Highbury to the area.

Highgate ⚫ Northern (zone 3)
This station has a low level station and an abandoned high level station. Interchange between the high and low level stations was available from 19 January 1941 until British Railways closed the high level station on 3 July 1954. The high level was to have become part of the Northern Line Finsbury Park to Edgware, High Barnet and Alexandra Palace 'Northern Heights' project, but this part of the project was shelved. The abandoned station above ground is still in situ. The low level platforms are served by Northern Line trains on the High Barnet branch and are unusual in having platforms that are much longer than the trains that serve them. This came about as part of a plan to ease overcrowding through the use of 9-car trains (the normal train length being 7 cars at the time). The platforms here and at Golders Green on the Edgware branch were long enough to accept 9-car trains, with the rear two cars only for the use of passengers travelling to Tottenham Court Road. At each station, the two rear cars would remain in the tunnels, but at Tottenham Court Road, the train would draw forward to allow passengers to alight from the rear two cars.

Hillingdon 🟣 Metropolitan 🔵 Piccadilly (zone 6)
Hillingdon was the last station to open on the Uxbridge branch on 10 December 1923 as Hillingdon (Swakeleys). The current station is slightly closer to Uxbridge than the original, which was closed to make way for the A40 Western Avenue, the new station opening in 1992. Although shown on the Underground map as just Hillingdon, the roundels on the station state Hillingdon (Swakeleys).

Holborn 🟠 Central 🔵 Piccadilly (zone 1)
The Piccadilly Line platforms were opened by the Great Northern, Piccadilly & Brompton Railway on 15 December 1906. The Central Line station however, did not open until 25 September 1933, in order to provide a much needed interchange with the Piccadilly Line. This resulted in the closure of the nearby British Museum station. British Museum does still retain its reversing siding, and at times of disruption, westbound trains may show Holborn as their destination, but will actually reverse at British Museum. On the Piccadilly Line, there is a junction here with the Aldwych branch which was served by a 3-car shuttle train at peak times up until its closure on 30 September 1994. The branch is still intact and is used for training and filming purposes. The Central Line platforms are numbered 1 (westbound) and 2 (eastbound), the Piccadilly platforms are numbered 3 (eastbound) and 4 (westbound), and the disused Aldwych branch platform is numbered 5.

A to Z Holland Park *to* Hounslow Central

Holland Park ● Central (zone 2)
A station that has been stuck in a time warp with signage dating back to the 1960s, Holland Park closed for replacement of the lifts on 2 January 2016 and is not expected to re-open until August 2016. While it is closed, it is expected that the platforms will receive a facelift, so how much of the old signage will remain when it re-opens is not known. The picture below is a last look at what the station was like before closure and shows the eastbound platform.

Holloway Road ● Piccadilly (zone 2)
This station still retains its Leslie Green designed station building. Access to the platforms is by lift and stairs only, and since Arsenal Football Club moved to the Emirates Stadium, this station is better placed for match day traffic than Arsenal is, and it struggles to cope with the crowds, becoming exit only close to match time. There is a second lift shaft here which was once home to an experimental spiral escalator, which didn't work and was never used by the public.

Hornchurch ● District (zone 6)
First opened by the London, Tilbury & Southend Railway in May 1885, Hornchurch was rebuilt in 1932 with two new platforms serving the District only. The platforms against the former LT&SR tracks became disused after 1962, but are still in place. There used to be a crossover to the west of the station that could be used to reverse trains at times of service disruption, but this was removed in January 2016.

Hounslow Central ● Piccadilly (zone 4)
Opened by the Metropolitan District railway as Heston - Hounslow on 1 April 1886 (the line through here had opened earlier on 21 July 1884). The station was renamed Hounslow Central on 1 December 1925.

A to Z Hounslow East *to* Kennington

Hounslow East ● Piccadilly (zone 4)
Opened by the Metropolitan District Railway as Hounslow Town on 2 May 1909 to replace the terminus of the same name and remove the need for reversing (see District Line history on page 50), the station was renamed Hounslow Central on 1 December 1925. The station building dates from a rebuild in 2002.

Hounslow West ● Piccadilly (zone 5)
Opened by the Metropolitan District Railway as Hounslow Barracks on 21 July 1884, the station was renamed Hounslow West on 1 December 1925. It remained as the terminus of the line after the Piccadilly took over from the District, until the Heathrow extension was built. In order to accommodate the new extension, the station had to be moved onto a new alignment, with the terminus platforms closing and new platforms opening on 14 July 1975. The station building is on the site of the old terminus and is linked the current station by a covered walkway. The station building dates from 1931 and was designed by Stanley Heaps in conjunction with Charles Holden.

Hyde Park Corner ● Piccadilly (zone 1)
Access to this station is by subway only. However, the original station building still survives and now forms part of a hotel. It is located opposite the eastbound bus stops close to the station entrance. It is easily identifiable by its Leslie Green red tiled façade.

Ickenham ● Metropolitan ● Piccadilly (zone 6)
Opened as Ickenham Halt on 25 September 1905 (the line through here had opened earlier on 4 July 1904). The current station buildings date from 1971.

Kennington ● Northern (zone 2)
At street level, Kennington is the only former City & South London Railway station to retain its station building complete with dome which houses the winding gear for the lifts. Kennington is

Kennington station, designed by T.P. Figgis and dating from the opening of the C&SLR in 1890.

A to Z Kensal Green *to* Kew Gardens

also the junction on the Northern Line where the two branches through Central London (Charing Cross branch and Bank branch) meet. Only a few trains via the Charing Cross branch run through to Morden, most terminate in platform 2, and then proceed round the Kennington loop to platform 1 and form a northbound train via Charing Cross. Trains via the Bank branch use platform 3 (northbound) and platform 4 (southbound). There is cross platform interchange between platforms 1 and 3 and between platforms 2 and 4 making it easy for passengers arriving on a southbound train from the Charing Cross branch to change onto a train heading towards Morden, or for passengers heading north on a train heading for the Bank branch to change onto a train via Charing Cross. There is also a central reversing siding to the south of the station, which can be reached by southbound trains from either branch, and any train leaving the siding can depart via Bank or via Charing Cross. Of note is platform 3, which is used by northbound trains via Bank. When built, the platform was on the right of trains as they entered the station. In order to accommodate the Charing Cross branch when it was extended to here in 1926, platform 3 was altered so that the platform is on the left as trains enter the station. The outline of some of the entrances onto the old platform can just be made out in the wall opposite platform 3 if you look carefully.

Kensal Green ● Bakerloo (zone 2)
The station is located at the London end of the 317 yard long Kensal Green tunnel. Opened on 1 October 1916, the platform buildings are of LNWR origin, but the station building at street level is a much more modern affair dating from 1980.

Kensington (Olympia) ● District (zone 2)
The Olympia branch is usually operated as a shuttle to and from High Street Kensington and only operates at weekends, Bank Holidays and when there is an exhibition taking place at Olympia. District trains use platform 1, while Network Rail trains use platforms 2 and 3. The Olympia end of the District's branch is single track, becoming double at Earl's Court Junction and then joining the District's Ealing Broadway and Richmond branch between West Kensington and Earl's Court.

Kentish Town ● Northern (zone 2)
Opened on 22 June 1907, Kentish Town still has its original Leslie Green designed station building at street level. Interchange is available here with Network Rail Thameslink services.

Kenton ● Bakerloo (zone 2)
Opened by the LNWR in June 1912, Bakerloo trains served the station from 16 April 1917. The station still retains its LNWR station building, platform buildings and canopies. There are no platforms here to serve the adjacent West Coast Main Line, and there never have been, as the station was built to serve the Watford DC tracks only.

Kew Gardens ● District (zones 3 and 4)
This station was opened on 1 September 1869 and today is served by both District Line trains and London Overground trains. Of note is the footbridge to the south of the station which dates from 1912. It still has high sides and smoke deflectors to protect those walking across it from soot and smoke from passing steam trains and is grade II listed. To the north of the station, the railway crosses the River Thames on Kew Bridge, one of only two locations where the Underground passes over the Thames (the other being Fulham Rail Bridge).

A to Z Kilburn *to* King's Cross St Pancras

Kilburn Jubilee (zone 2)
An island platform which serves the Jubilee Line. On the outsides of the Jubilee tracks are the northbound and southbound tracks of the Metropolitan, the trains of which pass straight by. The two tracks of the Network Rail lines in and out of Marylebone also run parallel through here. To the south of the station, the southbound Jubilee and southbound Metropolitan pass over the Kilburn High Road on an impressive steel bridge which has the words Metropolitan Railway in raised letters (pictured).

Kilburn Park Bakerloo (zone 2)
This station boasts a very fine grade II listed station building finished in red glazed tiles to a design by Stanley Heaps. When opened on 31 January 1915, the station formed the temporary terminus of the Bakerloo until the next section through to Queen's Park opened on 11 February.

King's Cross St Pancras Metropolitan Hammersmith & City Circle Northern Piccadilly Victoria (zone 1)
Not only this station a very important interchange between all the lines noted above, but also serves the main line termini of King's Cross and St Pancras International and also the Thameslink station at St Pancras. This station will of course always be remembered for the terrible fire of 18 November 1987 that claimed 31 lives. A memorial plaque and clock in the main ticket hall remember them.

A to Z   Kingsbury *to* Lancaster Gate

Look out for the multicoloured passageway to Granary Square (pictured right). There are several disused tunnels within the King's Cross complex, but as you depart eastwards from the station on the sub surface lines of the Circle, Hammersmith & City and Metropolitan lines, look out for a disused station. This dates from 1868, but was replaced by the current station in 1941.

Kingsbury Jubilee (zone 4)
Opened by the Metropolitan Railway on 10 December 1932, the station is today served by Jubilee Line trains on the Stanmore branch.

Knightsbridge Piccadilly (zone 1)
The closest station to the famous Harrods Store and the surrounding fashionable shopping district, Knightsbridge has always been a busy station, which is more than can be said for the nearby Brompton Road station which closed on 30 July 1934 due to low passenger numbers.

Ladbroke Grove Hammersmith & City Circle (zone 2)
Located on the Hammersmith branch, Ladbroke Grove opened as Notting Hill on 13 June 1864. It was renamed Notting Hill & Ladbroke Grove in 1880, and then to Ladbroke Grove (North Kensington) on 1 June 1919. It was given its current name in 1938. This station serves the famous Portobello Road market, and is also where the elevated A40 'Westway' comes alongside. The A40 parallels the Hammersmith branch from here to Westbourne Park.

Lambeth North Bakerloo (zone 1)
Opened as Kennington Road on 10 March 1906, this station acted as the southern terminus of the Baker Street & Waterloo Railway until it was opened to Elephant & Castle on 5 August of the same year. It was renamed Westminster Bridge Road on 5 August 1906, and then took the name Lambeth (North) from 15 April 1917. Finally, the brackets were dropped sometime around 1928. At street level, this station still retains its Leslie Green designed station building, while at platform level this station can be forgiven for looking a little unkempt. The platform tunnels suffer from more than their fair share of damp and water ingress which makes them look a little tatty. To the north of the station is a scissors crossover and a spur which leads to the Bakerloo Line's London Road Depot. Eleven trains stable here outside of traffic hours, but the depot is often empty during the day, except for a train of 1967 Stock that lives here for training purposes. Lambeth North is the station to alight at for the Imperial War Museum, which also just happens to be alongside London Road Depot, which can be viewed from the corner of Lambeth Road and St George's Road (the wall is a little high though…).

Lancaster Gate Central (zone 1)
Although not shown on the Underground map, this station is located within easy walking distance of Paddington mainline station, and if you are travelling along the Central Line with the aim of getting to Paddington, it is quicker to alight here and walk than to change at Notting Hill Gate onto the Circle and District Lines.

117

A to Z

London Road Depot outside of traffic hours with eleven Bakerloo Line trains, plus the train of 1967 Stock used for training (6th from the left, set back alongside the shed). The Shard forms an interesting backdrop as its illuminated top section is clipped by some low cloud.

A to Z Latimer Road *to* Liverpool Street

Latimer Road ● Hammersmith & City ● Circle (zone 2)
At the Hammersmith end of the station, the stub of the former Latimer Road Junction can still be seen. This is where a line branched off to Addison Road (Kensington Olympia). The line was damaged by a bomb in October 1940 and the line never re-opened.

Leicester Square ● Northern ● Piccadilly (zone 1)
The bustling West End station of Leicester Square offers an interchange between the Charing Cross branch of the Northern Line and the Piccadilly Line as well as serving the many pubs, clubs, restaurants, cinemas and theatres. The station has two station buildings at street level, one designed by Leslie Green and one designed by Charles Holden.

Leyton ● Central (zone 3)
This station pre-dates the whole Underground and was opened by the Midland Counties Railway as Low Leyton on 22 August 1856. It was renamed to just Leyton in 1868. The current station buildings date from 1879. The station and the line through here became a part of the Central Line from 5 May 1947.

Leytonstone ● Central (zone 3)
There are three platforms at Leytonstone which are reached by a subway beneath the line, which also acts as a public footpath from one side of the line to the other. The subway is decorated with murals celebrating the life of film maker Alfred Hitchcock who was born in Leytonstone. Also of note are two old advertisements that have been preserved (see below).

Liverpool Street ● Central ● Metropolitan ● Hammersmith & City ● Circle (zone 1)
Sitting proud at the west end of the eastbound sub-surface platform is a disused (and listed) Metropolitan Railway signalbox. As well as the current two sub-surface platforms, there also used to be a third (bay) platform for turning back eastbound trains. This has now been partially built on and covered up and it is difficult to see where this once was. Heading west on a train from here, look behind the signal box as you depart, and you can just see the top of the tunnel mouth that once led to the Liverpool Street mainline terminus, and which was used by Metropolitan Line trains from 1 February 1875 until 11 July 1875 when the current station (then called Bishopsgate) was opened.

The Central Line station was the eastern terminus of the Central from 28 July 1912 until 4 December 1946. There is a pair of reversing sidings in tunnel at the east end of the station, which only tend to be used at times of disruption these days.

A to Z London Bridge *to* Mansion House

London Bridge ● Northern ● Jubilee (zone 1)
The Northern Line platforms here underwent a major alteration in the 1980s when the southbound track was diverted into new tunnel, and the former southbound tunnel used to create additional space for escalators and a large circulating area in order to improve passenger flow (pictured). The Jubilee Line platforms here are part of the Jubilee Line Extension (JLE) and are fitted with platform edge doors.

Loughton ● Central (zone 6)
The station was designed by John Murray Easton and is Grade II listed. The station platforms have reinforced concrete canopies and wooden benches with roundel nameboards as seat backs. Some trains from Central London reverse here, usually in the centre platform. On the Woodford side of the station is a fan of sidings where ten trains stable outside of traffic hours.

Maida Vale ● Bakerloo (zone 2)
This station has Grade II listed status and is finished in red glazed tiles. It was designed by Stanley Heaps. Inside the station entrance, look up as you descend the stairs to the ticket hall and you will find two superbly restored Underground roundel mosaics. When the Bakerloo was extended through to Kilburn Park and Queen's Park, Maida Vale station was not ready and trains ran non-stop through here until 6 June 1915.

Manor House ● Piccadilly (zones 2 and 3)
Located on the Piccadilly's Cockfosters extension, Manor House has the plainest buildings of all the stations on this section of line, and they are the only ones that are not Grade II listed.

Mansion House ● District ● Circle (zone 1)
One of only two stations on the entire Underground that contains all of the vowels (the other being South Ealing). Mansion House was opened by the Metropolitan District Railway on 3 July 1871 and

A to Z Marble Arch *to* Mill Hill East

was the eastern terminus of the MDR's line until a further extension, opened on 6 October 1884, took the line to Mark Lane (completing the 'inner circle') and on to Whitechapel. The station currently has a three track layout, with a central bay platform used to turn back trains from the west, although this is seldom used these days.

Marble Arch Central (zone 1)

Located at the western end of Oxford Street, this station takes its name from the white marble triumphal arch which stands opposite, and which used to stand in front of Buckingham Palace. There is a reversing siding to the west of the station that can be used to turn back westbound trains, but this is only used at times of service disruption. The station is decorated by murals created by Annabel Grey as part of a renovation of the station in the early 1980s. There are 17 different murals throughout the station, one of which is pictured. This mural can be found on the westbound platform.

Marylebone Bakerloo (zone 1)

Opened with the name Great Central (the name of the railway company that served the mainline terminus above) on 27 March 1907, the station had its name changed to Marylebone on 15 April 1917. At the north end of the northbound platform, the name Great Central can still be seen in the tiles on the wall.

Mile End District Hammersmith & City Central (zone 2)

Mile End has four platforms; the centre two are used by the sub surface District and Hammersmith & City lines, while the outer two are used by the tube sized Central Line. This is the only place on the entire Underground network where cross platform interchange between sub-surface and tube takes place beneath the ground. The station was first opened on 2 June 1902 by the Metropolitan District Railway. The Central Line reached here on 4 December 1946, when that line was extended from Liverpool Street to Stratford. The name Mile End comes from a milestone nearby which marks a distance of one mile from the boundary of the City of London. The road was named Mile End Road and the station took its name from the road on which it is located, although the milestone itself is actually closer to Stepney Green station. Note the roundel above the station entrance which still says 'London Transport'.

Mill Hill East Northern (zone 4)

Served by a single track branch from Finchley Central, Mill Hill East is located on what used to be a through route to Edgware. Passenger services were operated by the LNER until September 1939, and the Northern Line began operating services from 18 May 1941. It was proposed that Northern Line trains would be projected through to Edgware, but this never happened, and the line was only

A to Z   Monument *to* Mornington Crescent

ever electrified as far as Mill Hill East. Freight trains continued to use the line to Edgware until 1964, after which the line beyond Mill Hill East was lifted. Despite being only a very short single track branch, the line can claim an Underground record, as it features the impressive Dollis Brook viaduct that stands 60 feet above the ground, the highest point above the ground on the entire Underground.

Monument ● District ● Circle (zone 1)

This station is linked to the large Bank complex and therefore offers interchange with the Docklands Light Railway and the Central, Northern and Waterloo & City lines. The station is named after the large stone Doric column which marks the spot where the Great Fire of London started in September 1666.

Moorgate ● Metropolitan ● Hammersmith & City ● Circle ● Northern (zone 1)

In the sub-surface part of the station, the abandoned platforms of the former City Widened Lines are still in situ, although now without track. There are two bay platforms here (3 and 4) which are used to turn back trains from the west. The area around Moorgate was heavily damaged during the war and was redeveloped in the 1960s, which involved rebuilding Moorgate station and covering it over with buildings. At a deeper level, Moorgate is served by the Bank branch of the Northern Line, and also by the former Great Northern & City Railway platforms which are now served by Great Northern class 313 EMUs running to and from Welwyn Garden City and Stevenage.

Moor Park ● Metropolitan (zones 6 and 7)

Opened as Sandy Lodge on 9 May 1910, the station was renamed Moor Park & Sandy Lodge on 18 October 1923. It gained its current name of Moor Park on 25 September 1950. There are four platforms here, with platforms 1 and 2 only used when the Metropolitan Line is operating fast services. The rest of the time, trains use platforms 3 and 4. Chiltern Railways trains do not call here. To the north of the station is Watford South Junction where the Watford route diverges from the Amersham and Chesham route.

Morden ● Northern (zone 4)

The station building here is a Charles Holden design in Portland Stone. With the development of surrounding buildings, only the front of the building is visible. There are three tracks through the station, but with platform faces on both sides of two of the tracks, there are five platforms. This is the most southerly station on the entire Underground, but the railway continues south of here to Morden Depot, making that depot the most southerly point reached by the entire Underground. To the north, just a short distance from the platform ends, the line enters tunnel. The first part of this tunnel is cut and cover, changing to tube tunnel at the north end of Kenley Road. If a train travels from Morden to High Barnet via Bank, it will be in tunnel for 17.25 miles until it emerges into the open at East Finchley, the longest continuous tunnel on the Underground.

Mornington Crescent ● Northern (zone 2)

The Underground map tells a little lie here, as it shows the Charing Cross branch through Mornington Crescent to the west of the Bank branch, when it is in fact to the east of it. The two branches cross over each other close to Euston. Mornington Crescent still has its original Leslie Green station building. When opened, passengers entered the lifts down to the platforms directly from the street, and exiting passengers were deposited directly onto the street from the exit lifts. Today, the position of the entrance lifts forms the main entrance to the station where ticket machines and the gateline are located. The current lifts are located in the position of the original exit

A to Z Neasden *to* Newbury Park

lifts, although passengers now enter and exit the lifts from inside the station building. The decorative grills above where passengers used to exit the lifts onto the street are still there and marked as '1' and '2' as seen in the accompanying photograph. The station was closed from October 1992 until April 1998 for lift replacement work, and at one time it was feared that the station might remain closed, but thankfully this did not happen. A memorial plaque to the late Willie Rushton is located in the ticket hall. Willie Rushton was a panellist on the BBC Radio 4 panel game 'I'm Sorry I Haven't a Clue' which often featured a game called 'Mornington Crescent'.

Neasden Jubilee (zone 3)

Opened by the Metropolitan Railway as Kingsbury & Neasden on 2 August 1880, the station was renamed Neasden & Kingsbury on 1 January 1910, and was renamed to just Neasden on 1 January 1932. The line was served by Bakerloo Line trains when that line took over the Stanmore branch on 20 November 1939 and Metropolitan Line trains ceased to call here after 1940. Metropolitan Line trains can still call here at times of service disruption, and S Stock marker boards are fitted at the platform ends. Look out for several fixed train stops on the Jubilee Line tracks. These are to prevent a wrongly routed Metropolitan Line train from proceeding along the Jubilee Line tracks.

Newbury Park Central (zone 4)

Newbury Park was opened on 1 May 1903 by the Great Eastern Railway as part of its Ilford to Woodford via Hainault route. Central Line trains, via the tunnel section through Redbridge from Leytonstone reached here on 14 December 1947, and then operated north of here from 31 May 1948 (although empty stock movements between Newbury Park and Hainault Depot had operated prior to this). The former GER line to and from Ilford was closed and lifted, although traces of it can still be seen at the Newbury Park end of the station between where the Central Line tracks part to go into tube tunnel. Several trains from Central London terminate here using the centre reversing siding on the Hainault side of the station. This siding is double-ended and is used in the autumn to reverse the Rail Adhesion Train after it arrives here from the Hainault direction. Newbury Park station still retains many GER features, and also of note is the Grade II listed bus station alongside the station entrance which features a copper clad barrel vaulted roof.

A to Z North Acton *to* Northwick Park

North Acton 🔴 Central (zones 2 and 3)
This station was upgraded in the 1990s, when the eastbound platform was converted into an island platform so that a third platform could be added. Today, platform 1 is usually used by westbound trains, and platform 3 by eastbound trains. Platform 2 is mostly used by trains that reverse here. To the west of the station is North Acton Junction where the West Ruislip lines and the Ealing Broadway lines split.

North Ealing 🔵 Piccadilly (zone 3)
Opened by the Metropolitan District Railway on 23 June 1903, this station still retains a fine example of a District Railway station building.

Northfields 🔵 Piccadilly (zone 3)
A four track station with a fine example of a Charles Holden designed station building. At one time there was a separate entrance to this station from Weymouth Avenue to the east, and the remains of a concrete walkway can still be seen at the east end of the station. At the west end of the station is Northfields Depot, one of two main depots on the Piccadilly Line. Beyond Northfields, the Piccadilly reduces down to two tracks towards Heathrow.

North Greenwich ⚪ Jubilee (zones 2 and 3)
A three platform station on the JLE, the centre platform is used mainly to reverse trains from Central London, of several are booked to do so. All platforms have platform edge doors fitted. This is the station to use for the O2 Arena and the Emirates Air Line, a cable car which crosses over the River Thames. There is also a large bus interchange here.

North Harrow 🟣 Metropolitan (zone 5)
This station was opened on 22 March 1915, but the current station buildings date from 1930

and were designed by Charles Clark. This station only has platforms on the local lines, with the northbound and southbound main lines passing alongside.

Northolt 🔴 Central (zone 5)
This station is located on the West Ruislip branch of the Central Line. It has a centre reversing siding which is used by several trains which are timetabled to turn back here.

North Wembley 🟤 Bakerloo (zone 4)
Situated on the Watford DC line, North Wembley is served by both Bakerloo Line trains and London Overground trains. The station still retains its LNWR station building and platform buildings.

Northwick Park 🟣 Metropolitan (zone 4)
Opened by the Metropolitan Railway as Northwick Park & Kenton on 28 June 1923, the station became just Northwick Park on 15 March 1937. The station consists of an island platform which is reached via a subway. The platform serves only the northbound and southbound local lines, with the fast lines passing by on the outside of the local lines. The two tracks of Network Rail's Chiltern line run parallel to the northbound fast. The station is located very close to where the West Coast Main Line, Watford DC line and Bakerloo Line pass beneath the Metropolitan and Chiltern lines.

A to Z   Northwood *to* Oakwood

Northwood 🔴 Metropolitan (zone 6)
Northwood station only has platforms on the local lines, with the northbound and southbound main lines passing by on the west side. Northwood has a reversing siding which can be used to turn back trains from the north. There is also a short stub siding which has been used in the past to remove redundant rolling stock for scrap.

Northwood Hills 🔴 Metropolitan (zone 6)
Like Northwood, this station only has platforms on the local lines, but was a later addition to the line, not opening until 13 November 1933.

Notting Hill Gate 🟢 District 🟡 Circle 🔴 Central (zone 1)
The sub-surface station served by the District and Circle lines is one of the finest stations on the Underground (as pictured). It has been sympathetically restored with replica old style lighting suspended from the roof. Interchange is available here between the sub-surface station and the deep level Central Line. Although the sub-surface station was opened by the Metropolitan Railway in 1868, and the deep level Central Line was opened by the Central London Railway in 1900, it was not until 1959 that the two stations were linked, both stations having separate entrances until then.

Oakwood 🔵 Piccadilly (zone 5)
One stop west of the Piccadilly's Cockfosters terminus, Oakwood has several trains start and finish their journeys here as it is located at the western exit of Cockfosters depot. Look very closely where the tracks enter the depot, and you will find a World War II pill box guarding the depot entrance. Opened as Enfield West on 13 March 1933, the station was renamed Enfield West (Oakwood) in 1934 and then to just Oakwood on 1 September 1946.

A to Z   Old Street *to* Perivale

Old Street ● Northern (zone 1)
Here there is interchange between the Northern Line (Bank branch) and the former Great Northern & City Railway. To the north of the station, the Northern Line turns to the west and passes through the abandoned City Road station which closed in 1922.

Osterley ● Piccadilly (zone 4)
Osterley was opened on 25 March 1934 to replace the former Osterley & Spring Road station, the abandoned platforms of which can still be seen at the east end of the station. The station building was designed by Stanley Heaps.

Oval ● Northern (zone 2)
The station building here dates from the 1920s, but a recent refurbishment has seen it given a rather modern appearance. When opened, the station was called The Oval and became just Oval in 1894. The station takes its name from the nearby Oval cricket ground.

Oxford Circus ● Central ● Victoria ● Bakerloo (zone 1)
This station serves the busy West End shopping district and the main subway entrances are conveniently located on the corner of Oxford Street and Regent Street. The original Central London Railway and Baker Street & Waterloo Railway station buildings still exist and sit on either side of Argyll Street and are used mainly as retail outlets, although there are exits from the station in each building.

Paddington ● District ● Circle ● Hammersmith & City ● Bakerloo (zone 1)
The sub-surface lines have two separate stations at Paddington, with Hammersmith & City and Circle line trains on the Hammersmith branch using platforms 15 and 16 alongside the mainline station. The Circle Line, along with the District Line, also serves Paddington (Praed Street) station which is situated on the west side of the 'inner circle' and still retains its overall roof. At deep level is the Bakerloo Line. The station here is on a sharp curve and the platform walls are decorated with a design celebrating the Greathead shield and the tunnel boring machine.

Park Royal ● Piccadilly (zone 3)
This station was opened on 6 July 1931 ready for the Piccadilly taking over the line from the District. It replaced the former District station at Park Royal & Twyford Abbey which closed the previous day. The station has a building which was designed by Welch & Lander, and which is heavily influenced by the work of Charles Holden. To the north of the station, the Piccadilly crosses over the top of the Central Line very close to Hanger Lane station.

Parsons Green ● District (zone 2)
Parsons Green was opened on 1 March 1880 as part of the MDR's extension from West Brompton to Putney Bridge & Fulham. Either side of the station are a number of sidings where 7 trains stable outside of traffic hours.

Perivale ● Central (zone 4)
Perivale has a delightful curved station building designed by Charles Holden which is a Grade II listed structure. The station building is at street level, with stairs leading up to an island platform.

A to Z   Piccadilly Circus *to* Pinner

To the east of the station, is the impressive 'Art Deco' Hoover building, which is now a Supermarket, but still very impressive to look at and very visible from passing trains.

Piccadilly Circus ● Piccadilly ● Bakerloo (zone 1)

The station ticket hall is well worth exploring with its circular concourse which retains many 1920s' features including 'Art Deco' style pillars and a linear world clock. Down at platform level, the station is decorated in cream, green and red tiles, offset with brown tiles on the Bakerloo and blue tiles on the Bakerloo. The station layout on the Bakerloo is quite unusual, as there is a section at the north end of the platforms where the northbound and southbound tracks share the same tunnel in order to accommodate a trailing crossover. At one time this open section had a scissors crossover. There are very sharp curves at the ends of the Bakerloo platforms – passengers are urged to Mind the Gap!!

The north end of the Bakerloo Line platforms at Piccadilly Circus with 3533 bringing up the rear of a southbound Bakerloo Line service on the left, and the Track Recording Train led by L132 heading north on the right. 22 December 2014.

The north end of the Bakerloo Line platforms at Piccadilly Circus with 3533 bringing up the rear of a southbound Bakerloo Line service on the left, and the Track Recording Train led by L132 heading north on the right. 22 December 2014.

Pimlico ● Victoria (zone 1)

The Victoria Line extension to Brixton opened on 23 July 1971, but Pimlico station did not open until 14 September 1972. It serves the Tate Britain, but is the only station on the Victoria Line that does not interchange with any other Underground or Network Rail line.

Pinner ● Metropolitan (zone 5)

Opened by the Metropolitan Railway on 25 May 1885, Pinner served as the MR's northern terminus until the next section to Rickmansworth opened on 1 September 1887. There are two platforms serving only the local lines.

A to Z Plaistow *to* Queen's Park

Plaistow 🟢 District 🔴 Hammersmith & City (zone 3)

The station buildings here date from 1905 and there are several platform canopy brackets with the letters LTSR cast into them. A bay platform at the west end of the station allows trains from the west to be turned back, but this is only used by a few trains. The Network Rail lines in and out of Fenchurch Street run parallel on the south side of the station. There are still platforms against these tracks, but they are disused and no longer cared for.

Preston Road 🔴 Metropolitan (zone 4)

This station has an island platform with platform faces only against the local lines. The northbound and southbound fast lines are located on the outside of the local lines, and the two tracks of the Chiltern line of Network Rail run parallel alongside the northbound tracks. The station building is located on Preston Road which crosses over the railway at this point. The station was opened on 21 May 1908 to serve the clay pigeon shooting venue of the 1908 Olympic Games. The current station however, dates from 1931 and is on the opposite side of Preston Road to the original.

Putney Bridge 🟢 District (zone 2)

Opened as the Putney Bridge & Fulham terminus of the MDR on 1 March 1880, it became a through station after Fulham Rail Bridge was opened in 1889. It was renamed Putney Bridge & Hurlingham on 1 September 1902, and then became Putney Bridge some time during 1932. The name Putney Bridge may be a little misleading as Putney is on the opposite side of the River Thames, and the station is in fact named after the nearby Putney Bridge which carries the A219 road over the River Thames. At the north end of the Fulham Rail Bridge adjacent to the station is a World War II pill box which was built to guard the railway bridge. Since the 2015 book, there have been a couple of alterations at Putney Bridge with the track in platform 2, and the large hydraulic buffer stop that it ended against both removed. This platform was only long enough to reverse trains of C Stock and could not accommodate the longer D Stock and S Stock trains. With the C Stock now withdrawn, there was little need for this track. The former bay platform is set to become the westbound track, and this change is likely to happen during 2016.

Queensbury ⚪ Jubilee (zone 4)

What do you do if you build a railway station in the middle of nowhere and that place does not have a name? Make a name up of course! This is how Queensbury got its name. The Metropolitan opened the station here on 16 December 1934 in what were open fields at the time in the hope that a station would attract residential development. As the name of the next station down the line was Kingsbury, the name of Queensbury was decided on. Of interest here is the roundabout opposite the station on which a large roundel is mounted.

Queen's Park 🟠 Bakerloo (zone 2)

Queen's Park is where the Bakerloo Line rises out of tube tunnel from Central London (or descends into it depending on your direction of travel). Alongside where the tracks rise out of the tunnel is the Queen's park South Carriage Shed. Outside of traffic hours, four trains stable here. The southbound and northbound Watford DC tracks to and from Euston are located on either side of the track formation here. Bakerloo Line trains can head towards Euston on these tracks, but only as far as Kilburn High Road empty to reverse. This is a rare move to witness.

The station has six platforms, two of which are located on the adjacent West Coast Main Line and are seldom used. Watford DC Line trains (now operated by London Overground class 378s) use platform 1 southbound and platform 4 northbound. Bakerloo Line trains use the two middle platforms (2 southbound and 3 northbound). To the north of the station platforms is Queen's Park

A to Z   Queensway *to* Regent's Park

North Carriage Shed. The Watford DC Lines pass either side of this shed, and the Bakerloo tracks merge with them on the north side of the carriage shed. The carriage shed itself has four roads numbered 21 to 24. Roads 22 and 23 are used to reverse trains that terminate at Queen's Park, while road 21 is used by northbound Bakerloo trains and road 24 is used by southbound Bakerloo trains. This means that passengers actually pass through the shed. Outside of traffic hours, all four roads can be used to stable trains.

Queensway 🔴 Central (zone 1)

Opened by the Central London Railway on 30 July 1900 as Queen's Road, the station was renamed Queensway on 1 September 1946. There used to be a reversing siding to the east of the station, but this has been removed and replaced (unusually) with a facing crossover. The position of vertical supports and tunnel walls did not allow enough room for a trailing crossover. It is only used to turn back trains at times of disruption, and can be used in both directions.

Ravenscourt Park 🟢 District (zone 2)

Although this is listed as a District station, and only District line trains call here, Piccadilly Line trains also pass through this station non-stop. The station was opened as Shaftesbury Road on 1 June 1877. It was renamed to Ravenscourt Park on 1 March 1888. To the east of the station can be seen the remains of the old Studland Road Junction where the line to Hammersmith Grove Road and Addison Road used to branch away.

Rayners Lane 🔴 Metropolitan 🔵 Piccadilly (zone 5)

At the London end of the station is Rayners Lane Junction where the Piccadilly and the Metropolitan join together. They then share tracks all the way from here to Uxbridge. Some Piccadilly Line trains terminate here and reverse using the central reversing siding at the west end of the station. The station was opened on 26 May 1906 and takes its name from a local farmer of the time. The station buildings date from a rebuild in the 1930s and were designed by Charles Holden and Reginald Uren. The picture shows the station platforms, station building and Rayners Lane Junction visible through the bridge.

Redbridge 🔴 Central (zone 4)

Situated on the Leytonstone to Newbury Park section, Redbridge is a mere 17 feet below the ground and was built using the cut and cover method with the tracks descending into tube tunnel at either end.

Regent's Park 🟤 Bakerloo (zone 1)

This is one of the quietest stations in Central London with only around 3 million passengers per annum starting or finishing their journeys here. There are no station buildings and access is via a subway entrance on the Marylebone Road. Although not listed as a connection on the Underground

129

A to Z Richmond *to* Russell Square

map, it is very easy to change from here to the Metropolitan, Hammersmith & City and Circle lines at Great Portland Street, as it is only a very short walk between the two stations. Very handy if you want to avoid the hustle and bustle of Baker Street.

Richmond District (zone 4)
Richmond station is served by the District Line, London Overground and Network Rail. Platforms 4 to 7 are all suitable for use by Underground trains and all are terminal platforms.

Rickmansworth Metropolitan (zone 7)
A fan of five sidings to the south of the station, two sidings to the north and number 23 siding alongside the northbound line to the south of the station (which can hold two trains) are used for stabling nine trains outside of traffic hours. The station is on a curve and at the north end there remains a water tower that dates back to the days of steam. At the south end is a bay platform which is not electrified, but is occasionally used to stable engineering vehicles.

Roding Valley Central (zone 4)
This is officially the least used station on the Underground with an average of less than 600 passengers per day. The station is on the Hainault loop, but it is very close to Woodford Junction where the Hainault loop splits from the Epping line.

Royal Oak Hammersmith & City Circle (zone 2)
Located alongside the throat of Paddington mainline terminus, the station is formed of an island platform serving only the Underground lines, but at one time it also had platforms on the main line too.

Ruislip Metropolitan Piccadilly (zone 6)
When the Metropolitan Railway opened its line from Harrow-on-the-Hill to Uxbridge on 4 July 1904, Ruislip was the only intermediate station. The station buildings date from that time. There is also a Metropolitan Railway signalbox at the London end of the station, but this hasn't signalled a train since the mid 1970s.

Ruislip Gardens Central (zone 5)
Located alongside RAF Northolt, this is the last station before the Central Line terminus at West Ruislip. Some trains start and finish their journeys here, as just to the west of the platform ends is the entrance to Ruislip Depot.

Ruislip Manor Metropolitan Piccadilly (zone 6)
Opened on 5 August 1912. The station sits on an embankment and is reached by stairs from the station building which is at street level.

Russell Square Piccadilly (zone 1)
At street level, this station still retains its Leslie Green red tiled building, while at platform level, it has a unique design of green and cream tiling. Leslie Green stations in the central area all had their own unique design of tiling to help the illiterate identify their station. Illiteracy was more common when the line opened in 1906.

A to Z St James's Park *to* Seven Sisters

St James's Park 🟢 District 🟡 Circle (zone 1)
This station entrance is incorporated into the grade II listed Portland Stone clad building designed by Charles Holden called 55 Broadway. This is currently the headquarters of London Underground, although LU are expected to vacate the premises soon. The building is then expected to be converted for residential use. At platform level there is some confusion…is the station St James's Park or St James' Park?

St John's Wood ⚪ Jubilee (zone 2)
Opened as part of the new tube line between Baker Street and Finchley Road on 20 November 1939 as part of the '1935-1940 New Works Programme', this station still retains much of the 1930s' character including roundels and the station name cast into the ceramic tiles along the length of each platform.

St Paul's 🔴 Central (zone 4)
Opened as Post Office, it is believed this name was chosen to differentiate it from the nearby South Eastern Railway called St Paul's. The SER station was renamed Blackfriars in 1937, and the Underground station took the name St Paul's on 1 February 1937. As the name would suggest, this station is conveniently located for St Paul's Cathedral. The westbound tunnel is situated directly over the eastbound tunnel here.

Seven Sisters 🔵 Victoria (zone 3)
This is where the line to and from the Victoria Line's depot at Northumberland Park joins the main Victoria Line. The station has three platforms, platform 3 is for northbound trains, platform 5 for southbound and platform 4 is for terminating trains from the south. Some

A to Z   Shepherd's Bush *to* Southfields

trains reverse just beyond the station using the tracks leading to and from the depot, while selected trains continue to Northumberland Park Depot as a staff special. The tiles in the seat recesses here depict seven trees which were known as the Seven Sisters and gave the area its name.

Shepherd's Bush 🔴 Central (zone 2)
The original terminus of the Central London Railway, this station has been a through station since the opening of Wood Lane station in 1908. Trains heading west from here go round the Caxton curve, which is the tightest curve on the Underground.

Shepherd's Bush Market 🟣 Hammersmith & City 🟡 Circle (zone 2)
This station opened at the same time as Goldhawk Road (1 April 1914) and replaced the former Shepherd's Bush station that was located roughly half way between here and Goldhawk Road. Until 2008, this station was just called Shepherd's Bush, but it was renamed to avoid confusion with the station of the same name on the Central Line.

Sloane Square 🟢 District 🟡 Circle (zone 1)
This station had an overall glass and steel roof, and the retaining walls and brackets that supported it can still be seen. The roof was destroyed in the war when it took a direct hit from a German bomb. Thirty-seven people were killed and the blast also destroyed the recently rebuilt station building and newly installed escalators. Passing over the top of the station is what appears to be a large green pipe. This carries the River Westbourne over the railway, a small tributary of the River Thames that starts in Hampstead and flows through Kilburn and Knightsbridge and into the River Thames near to Chelsea.

Snaresbrook 🔴 Central (zone 4)
Snaresbrook was opened as Snaresbrook & Wanstead on 22 August 1856 by the Eastern Counties Railway. It became a part of the Central Line from 14 December 1947, at which point it was also renamed Snaresbrook. The station still retains many 19th century features including station building and ornate canopy brackets.

South Ealing 🔵 Piccadilly (zone 3)
Along with Mansion House, South Ealing is one of two stations whose name contains all of the vowels. The station is on a four track formation which runs from Acton Town to Northfields (where it reduces to two). The two centre tracks are the fast lines, while the outer tracks are the local lines. The eastbound local also doubles up as a test track, and part way between South Ealing and Acton Town, a section of this line is fitted with water sprays to simulate wet weather conditions.

Southfields 🟢 District (zone 3)
The closest station to the Wimbledon Tennis Club becomes very busy during the Wimbledon Tennis Championships. The station's island platform is usually decorated as a tennis court during this period.

A to Z

A busy night scene at South Ealing with a train that will terminate at Northfields on the westbound local, a train for Heathrow Terminal 5 on the westbound fast and a train for Cockfosters on the eastbound fast. 25 October 2015.

A to Z Southgate *to* South Ruislip

Southgate 🔵 Piccadilly (zone 4)
The east end of the Piccadilly Line is above ground except for this station which is beneath a hill and is in a short section of tube tunnel. Looking west, it is possible to see a glimmer of daylight, but looking east the tunnel mouth can actually be seen (as illustrated). The station building is a circular 'Art Deco' design by Charles Holden with an illuminated 'Tesla Coil' fixed to the centre of the roof.

South Harrow 🔵 Piccadilly (zone 5)
Although a new station designed by Charles Holden was built in 1935, the original District Railway station building can still be found on the east end of the eastbound platform. At the east end of the station are six stabling sidings where four Piccadilly Line trains stable outside of traffic hours. The 2015 Guide Book advised of 9 cars of 1983 Tube Stock that was stored here. These were removed during 2015, and the cars taken away for scrap.

South Kensington 🔵 Piccadilly 🟢 District 🟡 Circle (zone 1)
Opened on 24 December 1868 by the Metropolitan Railway and the Metropolitan District Railway. The station today is served by the Circle and District lines at sub-surface level, and by the Piccadilly Line at deep tube level. The sub-surface station consists of one island platform, but it used to be much larger with seven platforms (inner rail Circle, outer rail Circle, a double sided Circle bay, eastbound District, westbound District and westbound District bay). There are still signs of the former layout with the retaining wall that used to support an overall roof, and a formation that is much wider than the current layout requires. The Piccadilly Line runs directly beneath the District and Circle lines and interchange between the lines is available.

South Kenton 🟤 Bakerloo (zone 4)
Consisting of a single island platform, South Kenton is served only by the Bakerloo and London Overground, although it is located alongside the busy West Coast main Line. The station was opened on 3 July 1933 and platform buildings are to a concrete and glass 'Art Deco' design. Access to the station is via a subway tunnel which also links the two residential areas on either side of the railway. Due to a lack of space, there are no ticket barriers at this station.

South Ruislip 🟠 Central (zone 5)
Situated on the West Ruislip branch of the Central, South Ruislip also has platforms on the adjacent Network Rail Chiltern main line and interchange is available here.

A to Z Southwark *to* Stepney Green

Southwark Jubilee (zone 1)
Southwark is on the Jubilee Line Extension and has platform edge doors fitted. Interchange is available here with Network Rail's London Waterloo East station.

South Wimbledon Northern (zones 3 and 4)
Despite the name, this station is actually in Merton and was opened on 13 September 1926 as South Wimbledon. It was renamed South Wimbledon (Merton) in 1928. The Merton in brackets was then dropped sometime in the 1940s. The station has a very attractive curved Portland Stone station building designed by Charles Holden.

South Woodford Central (zone 4)
Opened as South Woodford (George Lane) by the Eastern Counties Railway on 22 August 1856. The Central Line took over the railway through here on 14 December 1947, and the suffix was dropped sometime around 1950. Some of the roundels on the platform still show the suffix though. There used to be a level crossing at the Woodford end of the station, but this was removed when the line was electrified, severing George Lane. There is a station entrance on either side of the line linked by a footbridge which is outside of the ticket gates. There is also a public subway beneath the railway which links the two halves of George Lane.

Stamford Brook District (zone 3)
This station lies on the section of line between Hammersmith and Acton Town where Piccadilly Line trains run non-stop and only District line services call here. The eastbound fast (normally used by Piccadilly Line trains) does not have a platform face against it, but the westbound fast and westbound local run either side of an island platform.

Stanmore Jubilee (zone 5)
The northern terminus of the Jubilee Line, Stanmore also has a fan of sidings alongside the station where trains stable outside of traffic hours. The station was opened by the Metropolitan Railway on 10 December 1932. The original station building still exists at street level, however, the ticket office has been moved down to platform level to where a newer entrance from the car park enters the station. The addition of a third platform at Stanmore, which opened in 2011, has caused a slight anomaly, as the existing platforms were not renumbered, and as you enter the station, from left to right, the platforms are 2, 1 and 3.

Stepney Green District Hammersmith & City (zone 2)
A sub-surface station on the District and Hammersmith & City lines. There are one or two gems to look out for here. The westbound platform is fitted with a modern dot matrix indicator to tell

A to Z Stockwell *to* Sudbury Town

passengers the destination of the next trains, but the eastbound platform does not have a dot matrix indicator, and instead relays information to passengers via an old style light box (pictured). Also look out for the 'To the Trains' sign (pictured) at the top of the stairs leading down to the platforms from the ticket hall.

Stockwell ● Northern ● Victoria (zone 2)
This was the original terminus of the City & South London Railway until that line was extended in 1900 to Clapham Common. The site of the original terminus station was slightly to the north of the current Northern Line platforms, and is now the location of a trailing crossover. There is also a tunnel which branches off which used to serve the Stockwell Works and Depot. Trains used to reach this depot via a steep incline and were hauled up by cable, which was later replaced by a hydraulic lift before being taken out of use in 1924. In line with the opening of the Victoria Line through here in 1971, the station buildings were replaced with modern structures and cross platform interchanges were provided between the two lines.

Stonebridge Park ● Bakerloo (zone 3)
At platform level, Stonebridge Park is quite modern in appearance, but down at street level, the original station building still survives. At the north end of the platforms, two tracks branch to the right into the Bakerloo's Stonebridge Park Depot. Some trains terminate here and reverse in the entrance to the depot. Alongside the station at a higher level is Stonebridge Park carriage sidings where the Scotrail sleeper stock is maintained.

Stratford ● Central ● Jubilee (zones 2 and 3)
The Central Line is in tube tunnel at either end of Stratford station, but climbs up to serve platforms 3 and 3a (westbound) and platform 6 (eastbound). Westbound trains open their doors on both sides here. Stratford is the eastern terminus of the Jubilee Line and has three platforms located alongside the DLR's Stratford International branch at a lower level to the part of the station served by Network Rail and the Central Line. There is full interchange here between the Jubilee Line, Central Line, Docklands Light Railway, Network Rail, London Overground and local buses. The station also serves the Westfield shopping centre and Olympic Park.

Sudbury Hill ● Piccadilly (zone 4)
Opened on 28 June 1903 by the Metropolitan District Railway. The station was rebuilt in 1931 to a design by Charles Holden ready for transfer of the line to the Piccadilly.

Sudbury Town ● Piccadilly (zone 4)
As can be seen, the station is a typical Holden brick box with concrete lid. The interior and platform area of the station has also been restored to as near to original condition as is possible, and still retains many original features such as concrete canopies, lamp standards and footbridge, original glazing, old signage, a wall mounted barometer and an old news stand. Illustrated is an eastbound engineer's train hauled by L51 passing through the station on 13 December 2015.

136

A to Z

One of the finest examples of a Charles Holden designed station is at Sudbury Town. The picture above is not 1965, but 2015 when a group of photographers / vintage bus enthusiasts posed Routemaster RM1962 and Regent III RTL139 in front of the station outside of traffic hours.

A to Z Swiss Cottage *to* Tottenham Hale

Swiss Cottage Jubilee (zone 2)
Opened as part of the new Bakerloo branch from Baker Street to Finchley Road on 20 November 1939, Swiss Cottage retains many 1930s' features such as 'Art Deco' uplighters on the escalators and roundels cast into the ceramic tiles on the platform walls. The opening of this station, and the next station at St John's Wood, resulted in the closure of Lords, Marlborough Road and Swiss Cottage on the neighbouring Metropolitan Line.

Temple District Circle (zone 1)
Opened on 30 May 1870 as The Temple, the word 'The' being dropped sometime in the 1870s. The station is located on Victoria Embankment, with the railway running very close to the River Thames here. The station building is a fine example of an original MDR station building.

Theydon Bois Central (zone 6)
Opened by the Great Eastern Railway on 24 April 1865 as Theydon, it was renamed to Theydon Bois in December of the same year. The station became a part of the Central Line from 25 September 1949, when the Loughton to Epping and Ongar section was transferred over to London Transport.

Tooting Bec Northern (zone 3)
This station boasts two entrances on each side of a busy crossroads. Both buildings were designed by Charles Holden and are made clad in Portland Stone. The smaller of the two buildings, a subway entrance on the south side of the road, is a three sided building with a glazed roundel on each of the three sides. The station opened as Trinity Road (Tooting Bec) and received its current name on 1 October 1950.

Tooting Broadway Northern (zone 3)
This station has its very own safe door….not may stations can make such a claim! The site on which the station was built was once a bank. The safe door was too heavy to remove and so was left in position. It is in the escalator machinery room and not visible to the public. To the south of the station there is a centre reversing siding, used only at times of disruption nowadays.

Tottenham Court Road Northern Central (zone 1)
A very busy station, and busy interchange between the Northern and Central Lines. The station is still in the throes of a major rebuild to increase station capacity and accommodate Crossrail which is currently under construction. The Central Line platforms spent much of 2015 out of use, but they were re-opened towards the end of 2015. Some of the mosaics by Eduardo Paolozzi have been restored at platform level on the Central Line platforms (as illustrated on the next page), while other parts of the mosaics, that have been a feature of the station since the 1980s, have been removed and will be put on display at the University of Edinburgh.

Tottenham Hale Victoria (zone 3)
The tiled seat recesses here show a ferry (or 'hale') crossing the River Lea nearby. Interchange is available here with Network Rail.

A to Z

A train of 1992 Stock arrives in the westbound platform at Tottenham Court Road where the mosaics by Eduardo Paolozzi can be seen on the platform walls.

A to Z Totteridge *to* Turnham Green

Totteridge & Whetstone ● Northern (zone 4)
Opened by the Great Northern Railway on 1 April 1872 as Totteridge, it was renamed Totteridge & Whetstone exactly two years after opening. Today this station is part of the Northern Line's High Barnet branch, but it still retains its GNR buildings.

Tower Hill ● District ● Circle (zone 1)
The station has three platforms, the centre one being used to reverse trains from the west, several of which are timetabled to terminate here, usually District Line trains to and from Wimbledon. The station serves the nearby tourist hot spot of the Tower of London, and is also handy for Fenchurch Street main line terminus and the Tower Gateway station of the Docklands Light Railway. The current station opened on 5 February 1967 and replaced another station that was slightly further west and was originally called Mark Lane. There are still some remains of the old Mark Lane station still in situ.

Tufnell Park ● Northern (zone 2)
This station boasts a very fine three sided Leslie Green designed station building that occupies a street corner. The station closed in June 2015 for lift replacement work, but it is expected to re-open during March 2016.

Turnham Green ● District ● Piccadilly (zones 2 and 3)
Served by District Line trains throughout the day, Piccadilly Line trains also call here, but only from the start of traffic until 0650 Mondays to Saturdays and until 0745 on Sundays, and from 2230 every evening. The rest of the day, Piccadilly Line trains pass straight through without stopping. Just west of the station is Turnham Green Junction where the Richmond branch drops down towards Gunnersbury Junction. The eastbound District from Richmond passes underneath the District and Piccadilly lines to and from Acton Town so as to avoid conflicting movements.

The 2400 Heathrow Terminal 5 to Hammersmith service calls at Turnham Green during the small hours of 26 November 2015. Double ended 1973 Stock unit 858-658-859 is leading.

A to Z Turnpike Lane *to* Upton Park

Turnpike Lane ● Piccadilly (zone 3)
This station features a very large Charles Holden designed brick box and concrete lid station building with two large ventilation towers.

Upminster ● District (zone 6)
The eastern terminus of the District Line, and the furthest east that passengers can travel on the Underground. It is not the furthest east that the Underground reaches though, as trains can continue beyond the east end of the station to reach Upminster Depot. The District shares the station with Network Rail's Fenchurch Street to Southend / Shoeburyness line and London Overground's Romford to Upminster branch.

Upminster Bridge ● District (zone 6)
The railway here is on an embankment and is the only station between Barking and Upminster that is reached by a subway. Inside the station building is a reversed swastika pattern in the floor tiles (pictured). This was a common decorative pattern when the station was opened on 17 December 1934.

Upney ● District (zone 4)
Consisting of an island platform serving only the tracks of the District, this station was opened by the LMS on 12 September 1932, and has only ever had platforms against the District tracks.

Upton Park ● District ● Hammersmith & City (zone 3)
This is the station to alight at for West Ham United's football ground. Getting off at West Ham will result in a walk of over a mile. The station building which fronts on to Green Street dates from 1904. At platform level, the canopies still have LT&SR cast canopy brackets. The disused platforms are still in place against the Network Rail tracks.

A to Z Uxbridge *to* Warwick Avenue

Uxbridge ● Metropolitan ● Piccadilly (zone 6)

The Metropolitan Railway opened to Uxbridge on 4 July 1904. The original station was in Belmont Road roughly where a Sainsbury's Supermarket now stands. This station closed on 4 December 1938, and the current station opened on High Street the same day. The station has three tracks, but with platform faces on both sides of the centre track, there are four platforms. The design of the station is very similar to the one at Cockfosters at the opposite end of the Piccadilly, both of which were designed by Charles Holden. There are several things to note here, the stained glass windows by Ervin Bossanyi above the main circulating area representing heraldic associations of the area, the large clock and the 'next train' indicators by the entrance to the platform. There is a fan of sidings just outside the station where Metropolitan Line trains park outside of traffic hours. One Piccadilly Line train also stables at Uxbridge, but this stables in the station.

Vauxhall ● Victoria (zones 1 and 2)

Interchange is available here with local bus routes and the Network Rail station which is located on the main lines in and out of London Waterloo.

Victoria ● Victoria ● District ● Circle (zone 1)

Until 7 March 1969, the Circle and District were the only Underground lines serving this busy location which has a mainline railway terminus, a large bus station and coach station. From that date, the Victoria Line also served Victoria, initially as the southern terminus of the line, and then as a through station when the Brixton extension opened in 1971.

Walthamstow Central ● Victoria (zone 3)

The northern terminus of the Victoria Line. There are two platforms, with each line continuing for a short distance beyond the platforms where there is room to stable two trains outside of traffic hours. Interchange is available here with London Overground's Chingford line and also with several local bus routes. The tiles in the seat recesses here show an adaptation of a design by local textile designer William Morris.

Wanstead ● Central (zone 4)

Wanstead is the first station after Leytonstone on the line to Newbury Park. At the start of the war, this tunnel was built but not fitted out and it saw use as a bomb proof aircraft components factory operated by the Plessey Company. The first tracks in here were 18 inch tram lines used for transporting materials and products between the different sections of the factory. After the war, the tunnels were emptied of the machinery and the railway completed, eventually opening to traffic on 14 December 1947.

Warren Street ● Victoria ● Northern (zone 1)

Opened on 22 June 1907 by the Charing Cross, Euston & Hampstead Railway as Euston Road, the station was renamed Warren Street on 7 June 1908. The original station name can still be seen in some restored tiles on the southbound Northern Line platform. The Victoria Line opened to here on 1 December 1968 providing interchange between the Victoria and the Northern lines. The station is located at the top of Tottenham Court Road where it meets Warren Street and Euston Road.

Warwick Avenue ● Bakerloo (zone 2)

This station serves the 'Little Venice' area where the Regent's Canal meets the Grand Union Canal.

It is a simple two platform tube station with a sub-surface ticket hall and only subway entrances at street level.

Waterloo ● Bakerloo ● Northern ● Waterloo & City ● Jubilee (zone 1)

A large interchange that links the Underground lines of the Bakerloo, Northern (Charing Cross branch), Jubilee and Waterloo & City with each other and with the mainline terminus above. The Jubilee Line part of the complex is the most recent addition as it is part of the JLE and is fitted with platform edge doors. The Jubilee Line is linked to the Northern and Bakerloo lines via a long moving walkway.

Watford ● Metropolitan (zone 7)

The Metropolitan Line terminus at Watford is living on limited time: a new spur is being built to divert Metropolitan trains away from this terminus and into Watford Junction station instead. This is not likely to open until about 2020, but once this is open, the current terminus is likely to close to passengers and become just a stabling point instead. The station opened on 2 November 1925. The station building was designed by Charles Clark and stands at the end of an island platform serving two tracks with additional tracks for stabling trains either side. The picture shows the scissors crossover on the approach to the station with two stabled trains visible either side of the platform and with the station building visible in the distance.

Wembley Central ● Bakerloo (zone 4)

There had been a station on this site since 1842 when the London & Birmingham Railway opened Sudbury & Wembley. The Bakerloo didn't reach here until 16 April 1917 when the station was called Wembley for Sudbury. The station was renamed Wembley Central in July 1948. Today's station is a modern looking station which is located beneath office buildings, retail outlets and a hotel. There are also platforms here on the adjacent West Coast Main Line which are served by a number of London Midland and Southern services, and it is possible to interchange between these and the Bakerloo and also the London Overground service which shares tracks with the Bakerloo.

Wembley Park ● Metropolitan ● Jubilee (zone 4)

There are six platforms here, four for the Metropolitan and two for the Jubilee. The latter uses platforms 3 and 4 through the centre of the station with the northbound Metropolitan through platforms 1 and 2, and southbound Metropolitan through platforms 5 and 6. To the north of the station the Jubilee has a central reversing siding which has trains timetabled to reverse here. Alongside the southbound Metropolitan tracks are Wembley Park sidings where several S7 trains from the Hammersmith & City and Circle lines are booked to stable outside of traffic hours. Wembley Park signalbox also stands at the north end of platforms 2 and 3. At the south end of Wembley Park there is a complex of lines where the Metropolitan reduces from four tracks to two, and there is access to and from Neasden Depot, including a dive under which emerges between the northbound Metropolitan and northbound Jubilee. The station serves the nearby Wembley stadium and Wembley Arena and can get very busy when there is an event taking place.

A to Z   West Acton *to* West Finchley

21096 leads a Watford bound train into Wembley Park. The train is diverging onto the northbound Metropolitan local with the northbound Metropolitan fast in the foreground. Above the 2nd and 3rd car is the dive under to and from Neasden depot which is connected to both the Jubilee and Metropolitan lines. To the left of the dive under are the northbound and southbound Jubilee tracks, with the southbound Metropolitan and access to Neasden Depot on the far side. The two un-electrified tracks to the right of the picture are Network Rail's lines in and out of Marylebone.

West Acton ● Central (zone 3)
The station building here is a brick box with glass and concrete frontage designed by Brian Lewis and completed in 1940 to replace an earlier station building as part of the '1935-1940 New Works Programme'.

Westbourne Park ● Hammersmith & City ● Circle (zone 2)
The line curves through the station here to bring it alongside the Great Western Main Line. Until 1992, there were platforms on the GWML but these have now been demolished. Heading towards London, the Underground lines descend to pass through Subway Tunnel which passes beneath the GWML to emerge close to Royal Oak station.

West Brompton ● District (zone 2)
The West London Line has a station alongside the District here and it is possible to interchange between the two lines. On days when the District is not operating to Kensington (Olympia), passengers can change from the District onto a main line train here as an alternative method of getting to Olympia. Look out for the signs here that break away from the standard London Transport font and have the tops of the W on West Brompton crossing over.

West Finchley ● Northern (zone 4)
Although the High Barnet branch was opened by the Great Northern Railway on 1 April 1872, West Finchley station wasn't opened until 1 March 1933 by the London & North Eastern Railway (successor to the GNR). It became a part of the Northern Line when the High Barnet branch was transferred to the Underground on 14 April 1940.

A to Z

A Hammersmith & City to Barking Hammersmith & City Line service led by S7 21334 departs from West Ham against a backdrop of the City of London, 7 March 2015.

A to Z

The impressive modern architecture at Westminster with escalators leading to and from the deep level Jubilee Line platforms.

A to Z West Ham *to* West Ruislip

West Ham 🟢 District 🟣 Hammersmith & City ⚪ Jubilee (zones 2 and 3)
This station has a high level and a low level which cross each other at right angles. The low level runs north to south and consists of the Jubilee Line and the Docklands Light Railway's Stratford International branch. On the high level, which is on an east / west axis, are the Hammersmith & City and District lines, with Network Rail's main line in and out of Fenchurch Street running parallel. Interchange is possible between all lines. At the east end of the high level station is a central reversing siding which can be accessed from both ends.

West Hampstead ⚪ Jubilee (zone 2)
A station with an island platform serving the northbound and southbound tracks of the Jubilee Line only. Either side of the Jubilee Line tracks are the northbound and southbound Metropolitan lines. At the north end of the station, there is a central reversing siding, which can be used to reverse northbound trains (southbound trains can also go back into the siding).

West Harrow 🔴 Metropolitan (zone 5)
The only intermediate station on the Metropolitan Line's Uxbridge branch to be served only by the Metropolitan, with the next station Rayners Lane, and all stations between there and Uxbridge also served by the Piccadilly. The line through here opened on 4 July 1904, but West Harrow station was a later addition, not opening until 17 November 1913.

West Kensington 🟢 District (zone 2)
When opened on 9 September 1874, this station was named North End (Fulham). It was renamed West Kensington on 1 March 1877. At the east end of the station is a junction where a single line goes off into Lillie Bridge Depot.

Westminster 🟢 District 🟡 Circle ⚪ Jubilee (zone 1)
The original terminus of the Metropolitan District railway when it opened as Westminster Bridge on Christmas Eve in 1868, it became a through station when the MDR extended to Blackfriars on 30 May 1870. It was renamed Westminster in 1907. The station was heavily modernised to accommodate the Jubilee Line extension which opened through here in 1999. There is interchange between the sub-surface District and Circle lines and the Jubilee Line, and some of the modern architecture here is very impressive.

West Ruislip 🟠 Central (zone 6)
The western terminus of the Central Line consists of a single island platform serving two tracks. Parallel to the Central Line platforms are the Network Rail platforms served by Chiltern Railway's trains and there is interchange between the two lines. There is also a link between Network Rail and London Underground's Ruislip Depot which passes alongside the Central Line platforms. This link is used to deliver engineering materials and also the new S Stock trains when they are delivered from Bombardier. The large Ruislip Depot can be seen from the east end of the platforms. This depot is responsible for maintaining the Central Line fleet (along with Hainault) and is also home to the London Underground engineering fleet.

A to Z Whitechapel *to* Wimbledon

Whitechapel ● District ● Hammersmith & City (zone 2)
Whitechapel is currently a construction site as works associated with Crossrail are taking place. Once complete, the Underground station is expected to emerge with modern features and bear little resemblance to how it looked before the work began. The former East London Line, now part of London Overground, passes beneath the Underground station here, and there is interchange between the two lines. Between Whitechapel and Aldgate East there are traces of the former St Mary's Junction where there was a connection between the District / Hammersmith & City and the East London Line used to branch off. At one time this was used by passenger trains, but was latterly used only by empty stock trains; since the ELL has been transferred to London Overground, the connection has been removed.

White City ● Central (zone 2)
Westbound trains emerge into daylight here for the first time since Stratford. Right hand running occurs here (for reasons stated in the 'History' section of the Central Line). The station was opened on 23 November 1947 and replaced the former station at Wood Lane which was built to serve the Franco British Exhibition in 1908. It was this exhibition that gave the station its name, as most of the buildings making up the exhibition were white in colour earning it the nickname the 'White City'. There are three tracks through here, the centre track mainly being used by trains from the east that reverse here. There is also a reversing siding at the country end of the station. The tracks revert to left hand running via a flyover at Wood Lane Junction. At the London end of the station, inside what used to be the Wood Lane loop, were 16 sidings (which have now been built over). In their place on a new alignment are new sidings where 12 trains are scheduled to stable outside of traffic hours.

Willesden Green ● Jubilee (zones 2 and 3)
Opened by the Metropolitan Railway on 24 November 1879, Willesden Green's station building is a later addition from 1925, but still proudly displays the words 'Metropolitan Railway' in large letters just below the roof. Today the station is only served by Jubilee Line trains, but there are still platforms on the Metropolitan tracks which can be brought into use for Metropolitan Line trains at times of disruption. To the north of the station is a reversing siding for turning back northbound trains (southbound trains can also go back into the siding).

Willesden Junction ● Bakerloo (zones 2 and 3)
This station has a high level and a low level. The high level is served by London Overground services on the North London Line, and the low level is served by the Watford DC Line London Overground trains and the Bakerloo Line. The low level station consists of a large island platform with a central bay platform (which is only used by Overground trains). The station is in the centre of a complex of lines, with the West Coast Main Line running parallel to the low level station, the North London Line passing overhead, and connections between the high level and low level and with the Wembley freight yards. To the south of the station, there is also the Willesden Depot which is mainly used by London Overground.

Wimbledon ● District (zone 3)
Wimbledon has eleven platforms, which include two for Tramlink (10 and 10b), five for Network Rail (5, 6, 7, 8 and 9) and four for London Underground (1, 2, 3 and 4). All four of the District Line platforms are terminal platforms. There is a link between Network Rail and the District at Wimbledon North Junction just outside of the station, and Network Rail trains can run along the District tracks from here as far as East Putney Junction.

A to Z

A High Barnet to Kennington (via Charing Cross) service led by 51651 arrives at Woodside Park and passes the former GNR signalbox. 16 May 2015.

A to Z Wimbledon Park *to* Woodside Park

Wimbledon Park 🟢 District (zone 3)
Between Wimbledon and Wimbledon Park, the District runs along the west side of Wimbledon Depot, which is used to service the South West Trains fleet. Network Rail trains (South West Trains) can share the tracks with the District between Wimbledon North Junction, Wimbledon Park and East Putney Junction, where they can use a spur to travel to or from the Barnes to Clapham Junction line. These trains run empty along this stretch of line. The main line trains along here reflect the fact that the LSWR built the line, which did not pass into London Underground ownership until 1994. Wimbledon Park station consists of an island platform serving two tracks with a station building at street level above.

Woodford 🔴 Central (zone 4)
Woodford station has three platforms, with platform 1 being a bay platform. Alongside platform 1 are five sidings which are used to stable trains outside of traffic hours. To the south of the station is a reversing siding which is mainly used by trains that have arrived via the Hainault loop and terminated at Woodford, and are reversing to form a train back round the Hainault loop. Trains can also be reversed in the platform via a crossover at the Epping end of the station.

Wood Green 🔵 Piccadilly (zone 3)
This station has a turnback siding in tunnel for turning back trains from Central London. It is only used at times of service disruption these days. The station building was designed by Charles Holden.

Wood Lane 🌸 Hammersmith & City 🟡 Circle (zone 2)
Built in 2008, this station is located on the Hammersmith branch on embankment where the railway crosses over Wood Lane opposite the former BBC Television Studios. It is a very short walk along Wood Lane from this station to the Central Line's White City station, and this is shown on the Underground map as an interchange. When built, Wood Lane was built without a ticket office, which seemed unusual at the time, but which seems irrelevant now that ticket offices have been phased out across the Underground. There was a station at Wood Lane which opened as Wood Lane (Exhibition) on 1 May 1908 to serve the Franco British Exhibition. This was renamed to Wood Lane (White City) on 3 May 1920 and to just Wood Lane at some point in the 1930s. The station was last used on 21 October 1959, and then burnt down on 25 October 1959. The old Wood Lane station was slightly closer to Hammersmith than the current one. The new station has an old roundel from Wood Lane on display beneath one of the arches of the brick viaduct on which it sits, but this roundel is from the original Central London Railway station of the same name.

Woodside Park ⚫ Northern (zone 4)
Opened by the Great Northern Railway at the same time as the branch to High Barnet (1 April 1872). The station was originally called Torrington Park, and was renamed to Woodside Park on 1 May 1882. Today a part of the Northern Line's High Barnet branch, the station still retains many Great Northern Railway features, including the station building, platform canopies and footbridge. Perhaps the most remarkable survivor is the old signalbox on the north end of the northbound platform. It is no longer used to signal trains, but is kept in very good condition.

Opposite the signalbox is a large car park. This is on the site of what used to be the goods yard, and even after the Underground took over from the LNER, goods trains operated by the LNER and later BR, still served the goods yards at Woodside Park, High Barnet, Finchley Central, East Finchley and Totteridge & Whetstone until 1962.

References

USEFUL REFERENCES
London Underground Railway Society (LURS)
Membership of the above society comes highly recommended by the author. All members receive the excellent monthly magazine called Underground News which contains fantastic articles, colour and black and white photographs, up-to-date news from around the system, details of society events, features about modelling the Underground and regular fleet updates (which will help keep your London Underground Guide Book up to date). The magazine is worth the membership fee alone, but the society also organises occasional visits to Underground related locations, and there are the monthly society meetings that are held near to Great Portland Street station. These usually take the form of a talk by ex Underground staff, current Underground staff and management, photographers and historians.

More details can be found at **http://www.lurs.org.uk/**

Transport for London Working Timetables
Working timetables for all London Underground lines can be found on line at:
https://tfl.gov.uk/corporate/publications-and-reports/working-timetables
These can prove to be very handy for identifying workings, and for making sure you don't miss the last train home.

London Transport Museum
This site can be used to plan your visit to the London Transport Museum. Details of forthcoming events such as open days at Acton Museum Store, visits to abandoned stations and heritage train operations can also be found here, **http://www.ltmuseum.co.uk/**

Epping & Ongar Railway
A private railway operating heritage trains over a former part of the Central Line, the Epping & Ongar Railway is well worth a visit.

More details at **http://eorailway.co.uk/**